기초영어 1000문장 말하기 연습 3

박미진 지음

COURSE

TEACHING

SPEAKING

HI HOW ARE YOU?

WOW!

WRITING

LISTENING

HELLO!

ENGLISH

이제 지겨운 '공부'는 그만하고,
'연습'으로 말문을 틔우자!

기초영어
1000문장
말하기연습

토마토
출판사

이 책의 활용

Speaking Practice – 한국어를 영어로 전환하는 영작 연습

1. 한 페이지에 10문항씩 있어요. 한 문항을 보고 이해하는데 3초, 생각하고 말하는데 3초, 그래서 한 문항당 6초를 소비한다면, 한 페이지에 1분, 100문항을 10분 안에 만드는 연습을 할 수 있어요.

2. 강의를 들으면서 함께해요. 집중하는데 도움도 되고 이해하기도 더 쉬울 거예요.

3. 이제 혼자 말하면서 연습을 해보아요! 녹음기를 켜고 하면 나의 발음도 체크하고, 시간도 체크할 수 있으니 일석이조 이겠죠?

4. 이제 책의 맨 뒷장을 펴고 정답을 확인해 보아요. 강의 들으며 입으로 만들어 보면서 한 번, 글로 보면서 다시 말하면서 두 번, 답 맞추면서 세 번, 이렇게 한 문항을 세 번이나 반복할 수 있어요!

5. 시간이 있다면 마지막엔 글로도 써보세요! 만약 쓰기가 힘들다면 강의를 다시 들으면서 꾸준히 반복적으로 훈련해보는 것도 좋겠네요!

Review – 지금까지 배운 요소를 구분하는 연습

1. 여기는 처음부터 빠르게 변환하려고 하지 말고, 문장 속의 요소를 구분하는 연습이 필요해요. 한 문장씩 차근차근 읽어보고, 영어로 어떻게 말하는지 생각해보고, 천천히 말하는 연습을 해요.

2. 쓰면서 다시 생각해보는 연습을 해요.

3. 답을 확인해 보아요.

Dialogue Practice – 실제 상황에서의 응용

1. 영어를 먼저 읽어보아요!

2. 문장을 보면서 이게 배운 것 중에서 어떤 부분에 해당되는지 생각해봐요! (want to 인지, have to 인지 등등) 이렇게 구분만 할 수 있어도 너무 좋아요!

3. 영어가 익숙해지면, 뒤 페이지에 있는 한국어를 보며 입으로 영작에 도전해 보아요!

힌트와 하이라이트의 활용

힌트가 있는 문항이 있어요. 힌트를 보고 문장을 만들어요. 영어 문장을 떠올리는데도 도움되고, 적을 때는 스펠링도 도움이 되어서, 단어를 직접 찾아보는데 시간을 소요할 필요가 없어요!

하이라이트는 급하게 가지 말고, '잠깐!' 생각해 보라는 거예요! 조금 주의해야 답을 찾을 수 있으니, **하이라이트 부분**은 별표를 하고 자세히 봐주세요!

☐ 는 주어입니다. 네모 속 단어로 문장을 시작해 보세요!

목차

Unit 0 시작하기 1,2권 내용 복습하기   010

Unit 1 간략하게 요점만 말하고 싶을 때 '해, 하세요'   014

Unit 2 과거와 현재의 반전을 말하고 싶을 때 '예전엔 했었는데, 지금은 아니야' used to   040

Unit 3 과거 속 미래 의도를 말하고 싶을 때 '하려고 했었는데... (안 했어)' was going to   066

Unit 4 무언가의 존재 여부를 말하고 싶을 때 '있어/있었어' There is & There was   092

Unit 5 '존재'에 대해 더 다양하게 말하고 싶을 때 There has/have been & There will/might/used to be   118

Unit 6 의문의 문장을 또 다른 문장에 넣어 표현하고 싶을 때 '간접의문1 - 일반동사'   144

Unit 7 의문의 문장을 또 다른 문장에 넣어 표현하고 싶을 때 '간접의문2- be동사'   170

Unit 8 상대의 확인이나 동의를 구하는 질문을 하고 싶을 때 '하지, (그렇지)?'   196

Unit 9 '지금까지' 하고 있는 걸 말하고 싶을 때 '하고 있었어(지금)' have/has been -ing   218

Unit 10 상대의 의향을 물어보면서 허락을 구하거나 부탁하고 싶을 때 Do you mind?   244

정답체크   270

Unit

Positive (긍정)		Negative (부정)		Question (의문)	
I want to	~할래, 하고 싶어	I don't want to	~안 할래	Do you want to?	~할래?
I have to	~해야 돼 (의무)	I don't have to	~안 해도 돼	Do I have to?	~해야 돼?
I can	~할수있어	I can't	~못 해, 할 수 없어	Can you?	~할 수 있어? ~해줄래? (부탁)
You can	~해도 돼 (허락)	You can't	~하면 안 돼	Can I?	~해도 돼?
I will	~할게	I won't	~안 할게	Shall I?	~할까? (제안)
I should	~하는 게 좋겠다	I shouldn't	~안 하는 게 좋겠다	Should I?	~하는 게 좋을까?
I think I should	~하는 게 좋을 것 같아	I don't think I should	~안 하는 게 좋을 것 같아	Do you think I should?	~하는 게 좋을 것 같아?
I'd like to	~하고 싶어요	I wouldn't like to	~하고 싶지 않아요	Would you like to?	~하실래요?
I'm going to	~할 거야	I'm not going to	~안 할 거야	Are you going to?	~할 거야?

Positive (긍정)		Negative (부정)		Question (의문)	
I am -ing	해, 하고있어 (지금)	I'm not -ing	안해, 안하고있어	Are you -ing?	해? (지금) 하고 있어?
I 동사	해 (원래)	I don't	안해	Do you?	해? (원래)
I will	할 걸, 할 거야 (예측)	I won't	안 할 걸, 안 할 거야	Will you?	할까? 할꺼야? (예측)
I think I'll	할 것 같아	I don't think I'll	안 할 것 같아	Do you think you'll	할 것 같아?
I may I might	할지도 몰라, 할 수도 있어	I may not I might not	안할지도 몰라, 안할 수도 있어	May I?	해도 돼요? (허락)
I 과거	했어, 했었어	I didn't	안 했어	Did you?	했어?
I was -ing	하고 있었어 (그때)	I wasn't -ing	안 하고 있었어	Were you -ing?	하고 있었어? (그때)
I have p.p.	① 해봤어 (경험) ②했어 (쭉, 지금까지)	I haven't p.p.	①안 해봤어 ②안 했어 (계속)	Have you p.p.?	①해봤어? ②했어? (계속)
I could	할 수 있었어 (능력)	I couldn't	못 했어	Could you? Could I?	해줄래요? 해도 돼요?
I would	할 거야 (나라면)	I wouldn't	안 할 거야	Would you?	할 거야?

Unit

간략하게 요점만 말하고 싶을 때

'해, 하세요'

명령문으로도 많이 알려진 이런 짧은 표현들이, 명령 뿐만 아니라 조언이나
지시사항의 전달, 위험을 알리는 상황, 그리고 요청의 의미로도 사용 가능합니다!
간략하게 요점만을 전달할 수 있어 생활속에서 많이 사용 돼요.

Positive (긍정)	Negative (부정)
Do Eat } it. Say	Don't { do it. eat it. say it.
해 하세요 / 해주세요	하지 마 하지 마세요

해설강의 MP3

이렇게 만듭니다!

문장의 핵심 단어인 '동사'를 바로 사용해요!

Positive (긍정)	Negative (부정)
지금 가. Go now.	지금 가지 마. Don't go now.

<심화 표현>

단어가 동사가 아닌 형용사라면??

동사가 필요한 자리에 형용사의 절친 be동사의 원형인 'be'를 사용하시면 돼요.

예: 행복하세요! Be happy!

훈련용 MP3

정답확인 : P 270

01	이걸로 사. 좋은 가격인데.	
02	이거 입어. 이게 너한테 잘 어울려.	입다, 신다, 끼다, 쓰다 put-on
03	그거 해봐. 너가 좋아할 거야. 난 확신해.	
04	좀 먹어봐. 안 그럼, 이따가 배고파질 거야.	안 그러면 otherwise 배고파지다 get hungry
05	다 먹어요.	다 먹다, 끝내다 finish
06	생각해봐요.	
07	결정하면, 알려줘요.	
08	운전 조심(=안전하게)해요. 집에 도착하면, 전화줘요.	안전하게 safely
09	들어가기 전에, 신발 벗어줘요. 그리고, 모자도 벗어야 해요.	들어가다 enter, 벗다 take-off
10	하나 골라요. (넌) 어느 게 좋아?	

Speaking Practice

🕐 **1min**

긍정문

☞ 오른쪽 힌트를 이용해서, 직접 문장을 만들어보세요!

11	다시 고려해 주세요. 이건 좋은 기회일지도 몰라요.	다시 고려하다 reconsider 기회 opportunity
12	금요일까지 결정하고, 알려줘요.	
13	현명하게 골라.	현명하게 wisely
14	잔돈 가져요.	잔돈 the change
15	날 믿어. 이거 될 거야.	
16	날 용서해. 난 널 다치게 할 의미가 아니었어. (=진심이 아니었어)	뜻하다, 의미하다, 진심이 다 mean
17	이거 해. 네 차례야.	차례 one's turn
18	이거 가져. 선물로 주는 거야.	선물로 as a gift
19	계속해요.	계속하다 keep going
20	그거 그만 생각해.	그만하다 stop -ing

긍정문

☞ 오른쪽 힌트를 이용해서, 직접 문장을 만들어보세요!

21	그냥 둬.	두다, 내버려두다 leave
22	나 좀 혼자 둬. 지금은 혼자 이고 싶어.	혼자 두다 leave-alone
23	이거 만져봐. (=느껴봐, 촉감) 엄청 부드러워.	(손으로) 만지다, 느끼다 feel
24	다 (나한테) 말해줘. 알고 싶어. 너한테 듣고 싶어.	
25	뭐라고 말 좀 해. (너) 왜 이렇게 조용해?	
26	나 올 때까지, 여기 있어.	
27	그거 꺼줘. 지금은 뉴스 듣고 싶지 않아.	
28	그거 주워. 왜 떨어뜨렸어?	줍다 pick-up, 떨어뜨리다 drop
29	좋은 하루 보내!	
30	안전한 여행 되세요.	안전한 여행 하다 have a safe trip

31	조심해!!	잘 봐! 조심해! Watch/Look out!
32	멈춰!	
33	여기서 좌회전 해줘요.	좌회전 하다 turn left
34	이 지역들은 피해주세요.	피하다 avoid
35	이 약을 하루에 3번 드세요.	하루 3번 three times a day
36	눈을 감고, 상상해봐.	상상하다 imagine
37	진정해. 숨 깊게 들이 마셔.	진정하다 calm down, 숨 깊게 들이 마시다 take a deep breath
38	(너) 시간있을 때, 들러.	들리다 stop/drop by
39	이 파일을 설치하고, 컴퓨터를 다시 시작하세요.	다시 시작하다 restart
40	(그거) 잊어버려. (=극복해/이겨내)	잊어버리다, 이겨내다, 극복하다 get over

긍정문 Be

☞ 오른쪽 힌트를 이용해서, 직접 문장을 만들어보세요!

41	강해져. 넌 할 수 있어!	
42	조용히 해주세요.	
43	아! 살살해줘.	살살, 부드러운 gentle
44	조심해. 그게 다 끝나면, 전화해줘.	조심하는 careful, 끝난 over
45	더 나은 사람이 돼.	
46	긍정적이 돼. 넌 항상 긍정적인데. 왜 이것에 대해서는 부정적이야?	긍정적인 positive, 부정적인 negative
47	행복해.	
48	그냥 너 자신이면 돼.	
49	네 친구에게 잘 해줘. 서로에게 친절하게 해줘.	잘 해주는 nice to
50	영원히 내 사랑이 되어줘.	영원히 forever/ for good

부정문 Don't

☞ 오른쪽 힌트를 이용해서, 직접 문장을 만들어보세요!

51	내가 오기 전에, 아무것도 하지 마요. 🔊	
52	이거 쓰지 마. 🔊	
53	움직이지 마. 가만히 있어. 🔊	가만히 있다 keep/stay still
54	당황하지 마. 🔊	당황하다 panic
55	아무데도 가지 마. 길 잃어버릴지도 몰라. 🔊	길 잃어버리다 get lost
56	걱정하지 마. 다 괜찮을 거야. 이거 아무것도 아니야. 🔊	아무것도 아닌 nothing
57	이거 하지 마. 그거 안 하는 게 좋을 것 같아. 🔊	
58	아무 말 하지 마. 🔊	
59	그 애한테 말하지 마. 그 애 속상해 할 걸. 🔊	속상한 upset
60	나 기다리지 마요. 오늘밤에 늦을 것 같아요. 🔊	

부정문 Don't

☞ 오른쪽 힌트를 이용해서, 직접 문장을 만들어보세요!

61	너가 그거에 대해 확신이 없으면, 아직 하지 마.	확신이 있는 sure
62	무리하지 마. 나라면 무리하지 않을 거야.	무리하다 overdo
63	그거 포기하지 마. 절대 포기하지 마. 너의 꿈이 이루어질 거야.	이루어지다 come true
64	울지마. 제발 그만 울어. 나도 울거야.	
65	여기 동물들에게 먹이 주지 마세요.	먹이 주다 feed
66	여기서 수영하지 마세요.	
67	여기서 전자제품 사용하지 마세요.	전자제품 electronic devices
68	도움이 필요하면, 망설이지 마세요. 언제든지 제게 연락해도 돼요.	망설이다 hesitate, 연락하다 contact
69	그거에 대해 기분 나빠하지 마세요. 괜찮아요.	
70	그거 하기 싫으면, 하지 마. 난 그거 괜찮아.	괜찮은 ok with

71	웃지 마. 난 심각해.	
72	**오버하지 마.** (=과잉 반응 보이지 마)	오버하다, 과잉 반응 보이다 overreact
73	말 돌리지 마. 너의 대답이 뭐야?	말돌리다, 화제를 바꾸다 change the subject
74	**아무것도 만지지 마.**	
75	그거 먹지 마. 상했어.	상한 spoiled/rotten
76	그거 마시지 마. 유효기간 확인해 봐야 돼.	유효기간 expiration date
77	소지품 잊지 마세요.	소지품 one's belongings
78	**이 카드 가져 오는 거 잊지 마!**	
79	아무것도 하지 마. 너가 모든 걸 하지 않아도 돼.	
80	**나한테 그런식으로 이야기 하지 마.** (그런 말투로 말하지 마)	이야기하다 talk to 그런식으로 like that

81	불평하지 마.	
82	나한테 소리 지르지 마. 나 귀 안 먹었거든.	소리 지르다 shout/ scream/yell at, 귀 먹은 deaf
83	그냥 거기에 서있지 말고! 뭐라도 해 봐.	
84	나한테 뭐하라고 말하지 마. (이래라 저래라 하지 마) 내가 준비되면, 할거야.	뭐하라고 what to do
85	화내지 마. 너가 약속하면, 내가 너한테 말해줄게.	화내다 get angry/mad
86	네 자신을 탓하지 마. 누구의(=아무의) 잘못이 아니야.	탓하다 blame, 잘못 one's fault
87	놀라지 마.	놀란 surprised/ shocked
88	다른 사람들 놀리지 마.	놀리다 make fun of, 다른 사람들 others
89	그렇게 생각하지 마. 좋지 않아.	
90	너의 약점에 대해 생각하지 마. 너의 약점이 너의 강점이 될 수 있어.	약점 weakness, 강점 strength

부정문 Don't be

☞ 오른쪽 힌트를 이용해서, 직접 문장을 만들어보세요!

91	두려워하지 마.	
92	무서워 마.	
93	바보 같이 굴지 마.	바보 같은, 바보 같이 구는 silly
94	늦지 마.	
95	아프지 마. 특히, 내가 없을 땐. (여기에/네 옆에)	특히 especially
96	떨지 마. 넌 준비 되었어!	
97	욕심 부리지 마.	욕심부리는 greedy
98	슬퍼하지 마. 너가 슬퍼할 땐, 나도 슬퍼.	
99	그 애한테 잘 해주지 마. 그 애 못됐어.	잘 해주는 nice to, 못된, 너무한 mean
100	네 자신을 괴롭히지 마. 넌 잘 하고 있어!	자신을 괴롭히는 hard on oneself

Review

복습강의 MP3

Positive (긍정)	Negative (부정)	Question (의문)
Do/Go ···. [동사 바로]	Don't	-
해, 하세요	하지 마, 하지 마세요	-

01	여기 앉으셔도 돼요.
02	우리 저기에 앉는 게 좋을 것 같아.
03	여기에 앉아야 돼. 여기에 앉고 싶어.
04	너랑 여기에 앉을 게.
05	난 친구랑 저기에 앉을 거야. 이따 봐.
06	누군가가 여기에 앉아요. (자리 있어요)
07	그 애는 항상 나랑 같이 앉아. 이 자리 맡아 놔야 돼. 그 애 금방 올 거야.
08	내가 거기 갔을 땐, 누군가 거기 앉아 있었어.
09	난 그냥 거기에 앉아 있었어. 뭐라고 말할지 모르겠더라고.
10	여기 앉으세요.
11	그 애가 여기에 앉을지도 몰라. 그 앤 보통 여기 앉더라고.
12	나라면 저기에 앉을 거야. 좋은 자리야.
13	우리 같이 앉을 수 있어.
14	너랑 같이 앉아서 좋다.
15	우리 여기 앉지 뭐.

정답확인 : P 274

16	우리 오늘은 같이 앉지 않는 게 좋겠다.
17	난 그 애랑 앉지 않을 것 같아.
18	오늘은 거기 앉지 않을 거야. 난 그 자리 별로야. [그 자리 that/the seat]
19	거기 앉지 마. 젖었어.
20	난 내 친구랑 안 앉을 수도 있어. 내 친구 오늘 안 올 것 같아.
21	우리 여기 앉지 않아도 돼. 너가 원하지 않으면.
22	그 앤 혼자 앉지 않을 것 같아.
23	저 여기 앉는 거 아니에요. 가져가도 돼요. 전 저기에 앉아요.
24	그 앤 혼자 앉지 않아. 항상 친구들이랑 있어. 그 앤 친구가 많아.
25	나 혼자 앉지 않았어.
26	그 애랑 같이 못 앉았어. 그 앤 늦게 왔어.
27	난 여기 안 앉을래.
28	저 여기 앉아도 되나요?
29	어디 앉을래?
30	나랑 여기 앉아줄래? 너랑 이야기하고 싶어.

31	저희 여기 앉아야 되나요?
32	우리 여기 앉는 게 좋을까?
33	넌 어디 앉아? 너의 자리가 어디야? (지금)
34	저기에 앉아봤어?
35	어디에 앉았었어?
36	Tim은 어디에 앉아요? 그 애의 자리는 어디예요? (원래)
37	저희 어디에 앉을 수 있어요? 같이 앉을 수 있을까요?
38	우리 어디 앉을까?
39	너라면 어디에 앉겠어?
40	어디 앉을 거야?
41	난 이번 건 빠질래. 이거 할 시간이 없을 것 같아. [이번 것 this one]
42	난 이번엔 빠질 거야.
43	너 피곤하면, 이번 건 빠져도 돼.
44	전 이번 것은 빠져야겠어요.

레시피

How to make instant noodles

1. Choose/Pick your favorite instant noodles.

2. Put 2 cups of water in a pot/saucepan.

3. Boil the water.

4. Put the noodles in the boiling water.

5. Add/Put the seasoning (packets).

6. Stir the noodles.

7. Cook the noodles for 3 or 4 minutes.

8. If you want, you can add an egg or some spring/green onions.

9. Pour the noodles in a bowl.

10. Enjoy!

How to cook fried eggs / How to fry an egg

1. Put some oil in a pan/frying pan.

2. Heat the oil.

3. Crack/Break an egg in(to) the pan.

4. Wait for the egg to cook.

For sunny side up / over easy / over hard

1. Heat some oil in a pan/frying pan.

2. Break/Crack an egg in (to) the pan.

3. Cover the pan with a lid.

4. Cook/Leave for 3 minutes.

5. Turn/Flip over and cook for 30 seconds for over easy eggs.

6. Turn/Flip over and cook for 2 minutes for over hard eggs.

7. Sprinkle/Season with salt and pepper.

라면 끓이는(=만드는) 법

1. 가장 좋아하는 라면을 고른다.

2. 냄비에 물 두 컵을 넣는다.

3. 물을 끓인다.

4. 끓는 물에 라면을 넣는다.

5. 스프 [seasoning (packets)]를 첨가한다.

6. 면을 젓는다. [젓다 stir]

7. 면을 3분이나 4분간 익힌다.

8. 원하면, 계란이나 파를 첨가해도 된다. [첨가하다 add]

9. 그릇에 라면을 따른다. [따르다 pour]

10. 즐긴다.

계란 후라이 요리하는 법

1. 팬에 기름을 넣어요.

2. 그 기름을 달궈요. [데우다 heat]

3. 팬에 계란을 깨요.

4. 계란이 익기를 기다려요.

반숙/ 완숙 계란 요리

1. 팬에 기름을 달궈요.

2. 팬에 계란을 깨요.

3. 뚜껑으로 팬을 덮어요.

4. 3분 동안 두어요.

5. 반숙을 위해서는 뒤집고, 30초 동안 요리해요. [뒤집다 flip over]

6. 완숙을 위해서는 뒤집고, 2분 동안 요리해요.

7. 소금과 후추를 뿌려요. [뿌리다 sprinkle/season with]

How to boil eggs

1. Place/Put eggs in a pot/saucepan.

2. Fill the pot/pan with cold water.

3. Cover the pot/pan with a lid.

4. Boil for 7 minutes for soft boiled eggs.

5. Boil for 12 minutes for hard boiled eggs.

6. Put the eggs in cold water to cool.

7. Peel the eggs and enjoy!

A: How do you like your eggs?

B: I'd like (to have) scrambled eggs, please.

-

A: How would you like your eggs?

B: I'd like my eggs poached, please. (/ Can/could I have poached eggs, please?)

-

A: How would you like your eggs?

B: I'll have fried eggs, please. Can you make it over hard?

-

A: How do you want your egg(s) this morning?

B: I want (/I'd like) over easy, please.

B: I'll have sunny side up.

레시피

계란 삶는 법

1. 냄비에 계란을 넣어요.

2. 찬물로 냄비를 채워요.

3. 뚜껑으로 냄비를 덮어요.

4. 반숙을 위해서는 7분 동안 끓여요.

5. 완숙을 위해서는 12분 동안 끓여요.

6. 식게 찬물에 계란을 넣어요.

7. 계란 껍질을 벗기고[peel], 즐겨요!

A: 어떤 계란이 좋아요? [How do you like your eggs?]

B: 스크램블로 먹고 싶어요.

-

A: 계란 어떻게 해드릴까요? [How would you like ~?]

B: 수란으로 해주세요. [I'd like my eggs~, please]

-

A: 계란 어떻게 해드릴까요?

B: 계란 후라이로 할게요. 완숙으로 만들어 줄 수 있어요?

-

A: 오늘 아침 어떤 계란을 원하세요?

B: 반숙을 원해요.

B: Sunny side up으로 할게요.

· Boiled eggs (삶은 계란)
  soft boiled (반숙)
  hard boiled (완숙)

· Fried eggs (계란 후라이)
  sunny side up, over easy (반숙)
  over medium, over hard (완숙)

· Poached eggs (수란)

· Scrambled eggs (스크램블)

Unit

2

과거와 현재의 반전을 말하고 싶을 때

'예전엔 했었는데, 지금은 아니야' used to

과거에 한 일에 속하긴 하지만, 'used to'는 그 과거와 현재가 반대라는 의미까지 내포하고 있어요. 그래서 이 표현에는 과거의 표현인 '예전에, 옛날엔, 전에는'이라는 시간적 요소와, '하지만 지금은'이라는 반전 요소가 함께 들어가 있어요.

따라서 이 표현은 지난 과거와 지금을 비교하여 표현함으로써, 하고 싶은 말을 더 정확하게 전달할 수 있어서 활용도가 매우 높은 표현입니다.

Positive (긍정)	Negative (부정)	Question (의문)
I used to	I didn't use to	Did you use to?
옛날엔 했었는데… (지금은 안 해)	옛날엔 안 했었는데… (지금은 해)	옛날엔 했었어?

이렇게 만듭니다!

문장의 핵심 단어인 '동사'를 넣습니다.

Positive (긍정)	Negative (부정)	Question (의문)
옛날엔 거기 매일 갔었는데… (지금은 안가)	예전엔 거기 안 다녔었어… (지금은 다녀)	넌 예전에 어디 다녔었어?
I used to go there every day.	I didn't use to go there.	Where did you use to go?

긍정문 I used to
☞ 오른쪽 힌트를 이용해서, 직접 문장을 만들어보세요!

훈련용 MP3

정답확인 : P 275

01	난 예전에 머리가 길었었어.	머리가 길다 have long hair
02	그 앤 예전에 머리가 짧았었어.	머리가 짧다 have short hair
03	그 앤 예전에 술을 많이 마셨었어.	
04	그 앤 예전에 담배를 많이 폈었어. 5년 전에 담배 끊었어.	끊다 quit/stop -ing
05	나 예전엔 거기 자주 갔었는데. 안 가본지 오래 됐다.	
06	우리 예전에 여기 자주 왔었어. 이게 우리가 가장 좋아하는 장소였어.	가장 좋아하는 곳 one's favorite place/spot
07	난 예전에 우유를 절대 안 마셨었어. I never	
08	난 예전에 이거 자주 먹었었는데. 지금은 별로야.	별로다 = 안 좋아하다
09	난 예전엔 공부를 절대 열심히 안 했었는데. 난 공부하는 거 좋아해.	좋아하다 like/love -ing
10	Jim은 예전엔 야채를 절대 안 먹었었어. 지금은 야채 좋아해.	

11	내가 어렸을 땐, 이거 아주 좋아했었는데… 매일 매일 하고 싶었어.	
12	난 예전에 커피를 많이 마셨었는데… 이젠 차가 더 좋아.	더 좋아하다, 선호하다 prefer
13	Mark는 예전에 공항에서 일했었는데, 지금은 트럭 운전해.	
14	나도 옛날엔 그거 있었는데. 몇 년 전에 잃어버렸어. 그거 잃어버렸을 때, 잠도 못 잤어.	
15	나 옛날엔 여기서 일했었어. 지금은 강남에서 일해.	
16	난 예전엔 그 애 싫어했었어. 난 그 앨 오해했었어.	오해하다 misunderstand
17	우리 옛날엔 강남에 살았었어. 지금은 일산에 살아. 작년에 이사했어.	
18	우리 예전엔 극장에 자주 가곤 했었는데…	
19	우리 예전엔 같이 일했었어. 그 애 내 동료였어.	동료 coworker/ colleague
20	나 옛날엔 여행을 많이 다녔었는데… 요즘 여행할 시간이 없었어.	

Speaking Practice

1min

긍정문 I used to
☞ 오른쪽 힌트를 이용해서, 직접 문장을 만들어보세요!

21	우리 어렸을 땐, 내 동생이랑 난 늘 싸웠었어.	늘 all the time
22	너 옛날에는 나한테 매일 전화했었잖아. 많이 변했어.	변하다, 바뀌다 change
23	너 예전엔 이거 좋아했었잖아. 내가(내 말이) 틀려?	
24	나 예전엔 그거 많이 했었는데… 그거 하는 거 좋아했었어.	
25	나도 예전엔 그 앨 믿었었지… 더 이상은 안 믿어.	
26	그 애 예전엔 멋져 보였었는데. 매우 잘생겼었지…	
27	나 예전엔 이 노래 매일 들었었어. 그 땐 이게 내가 가장 좋아하는 노래 였어.	그 땐 (back) then
28	우리 예전엔 서로 매일 통화했었는데…	통화하다 talk to
29	나도 예전엔 그렇게 믿었었어.	
30	많은 사람들이 예전엔 그걸 봤어. 지금은 다르지만.	

긍정문 I used to
☞ 오른쪽 힌트를 이용해서, 직접 문장을 만들어보세요!

31	우리 예전엔 매일 서로 봤었는데. 너 안 본지 오래됐다. 어떻게 지냈어?	
32	나 이거 예전엔 모았었어.	모으다, 수집하다 collect
33	나 예전엔 여기다 돈 많이 썼었지.	(돈) 쓰다 spend (a lot of) money on
34	부모님들이 예전엔 그들의 아이들을 위해 모든 것을 다 했었지.	
35	많은 사람들이 예전엔 (그들의) 가족과 시간을 보냈었어.	시간을 보내다 spend time with
36	모두가 예전엔 이걸 갖고 싶어했어. 인기 많았었지. 나도 갖고 싶어했었어.	인기 많은 popular
37	모두가 예전엔 이걸 갖고 있었어, 나만 빼고.	빼고, 제외하고 except
38	이거 예전엔 정말 오래 걸렸었지. (그게) 영원처럼 느껴졌었어.	~처럼 느끼다 feel like
39	이거 예전엔 아무것도 안 들었었어. (돈이)	아무것도 nothing
40	정말 많은 사람들이 예전엔 가난했었어.	가난한 poor

긍정문 I used to be

☞ 오른쪽 힌트를 이용해서, 직접 문장을 만들어보세요!

41	나 학생 땐, 굉장히 소심했었어.	소심한 shy
42	그 애 어렸을 땐, 활발했었는데…	활발한 outgoing
43	Kate는 예전에 선생님이었어.	
44	나 이거 옛날엔 잘 했었는데.	잘하는 good at
45	우리 예전엔 서로 가까웠는데… 시간이 어디로 갔지?	가까운 close to
46	너 예전엔 내 편이었잖아. 내 편들어!	편 on one's side
47	그 애가 예전에 내 가장 친한 친구였어. 우린 정말 친한 친구였었지.	
48	돈이 예전엔 나한테 아주 중요했었지. 아직도 중요하긴 하지만, 그게 전부는 아니야.	전부 everything
49	예전엔 사람이 많았는데. 오늘은 조용하네.	사람이 많은, 붐비는 crowded
50	그거 예전엔 좋았는데… 지금은 (그게) 다르게 느껴져.	

51	이거 예전엔 아주 비쌌었어.	
52	그거 예전엔 여기 있었는데…	
53	이게 옛날엔 학교였어. 지금은 병원이지만.	
54	그게 예전엔 내가 가장 좋아하는 거였는데…	가장 좋아하는 것 one's favorite
55	그거 예전엔 아주 컸었어.	
56	이게 예전엔 인기가 많았었는데.	인기가 많은 popular
57	그거 예전엔 거기에 있었어.	
58	그거 예전엔 위험했었는데… 지금은 아니야.	
59	그게 옛날엔 문제 였는데… 지금은 문제가 아니야.	
60	이거 내꺼였는데. 내 동생한테 줬어.	

61	나 예전엔 여기에 살지 않았었어. 혼자 살았었어.	
62	난 예전엔 그 애랑 같이 일하지 않았었어.	
63	나 예전엔 해산물 안 먹었었어. 근데 지금은 먹을 수 있어.	
64	우리 예전엔 서로 안 좋아했었는데. 지금은 좋은 친구야.	
65	그 애 예전엔 울지 않았었는데. 지금은 많이 울어.	
66	우리 예전엔 여기 잘 안 왔었어. 근데 지금은 매주 월요일 마다 와.	매주 월요일 every Monday
67	나 예전엔 이거 안 썼어… 솔직히, 못 썼지. 어떻게 쓰는 건지 몰랐어.	
68	그 애 예전엔 나한테 아무것도 말하지 않았었는데. 지금은 모든 걸 나한테 말해주고 싶어해. 말이 많아졌어.	말이 많아지다 become chatty/talkative
69	너 예전엔 이거 없었잖아. 언제 샀어?	
70	나 옛날엔 머리가 길지 않았어. 내 머리 지금은 길어.	

부정문 I didn't use to

☞ 오른쪽 힌트를 이용해서, 직접 문장을 만들어보세요!

71	사람들이 예전엔 이거에 대해 몰랐지.	
72	너 예전엔 잘 안 웃었는데… 너의 미소 보는 거 좋다.	
73	예전엔 돈이 많이 들지 않았었는데… 그때가 그립다.	그때, 그 날들, 그 시간들 those days
74	이거 예전엔 이렇게 오래 걸리지 않았었는데… 이상하네.	
75	그 애 예전엔 이기적이지 않았는데. 사려 깊었었는데.	이기적인 selfish, 사려깊은 thoughtful/ considerate
76	이거 예전엔 여기 없었는데.	
77	옛날엔 이렇게 비싸지 않았는데. 가격이 올랐어.	오르다 go up
78	나 학생 땐, 자신감이 없었었어.	자신감 있는 confident
79	이거 옛날엔 안 이랬는데… 너무 많이 변했어.	이런, 이런 식인 like this
80	이거 옛날엔 어렵지 않았는데. 언제 (이게) 이렇게 어려워졌지?	어려워지다 get/ become hard(er)

의문문 Did you use to

☞ 오른쪽 힌트를 이용해서, 직접 문장을 만들어보세요!

81	너 예전엔 어디에서 살았었어?	
82	누구랑 살았어?혼자서 살았었니?	
83	너 이거 예전엔 좋아했었니? 이것들 많이 있네.	이것들 많이 (so) many of them
84	너 이거 예전에 수집했었어? 얼마나 오래 이거 수집했어?	모으다, 수집하다 collect
85	예전에 어디서 일했었어? 거기서 얼마나 일했어?	
86	너 어렸을 땐, 뭘 좋아했었어?	
87	예전에 여기 얼마나 자주 왔었어?	
88	그 앤 예전에 여행을 많이 했었어?	
89	학생일 때, 교복 입었었어?	교복 a school uniform
90	기분 다운 되었을 땐, 넌 뭘 했었어?	

의문문 Did it use to
☞ 오른쪽 힌트를 이용해서, 직접 문장을 만들어보세요!

91	옛날엔 거기 가는데 일주일 걸렸었어? 너무 오래 걸렸다.	
92	예전엔 얼마나 오래 걸렸어?	
93	예전엔 얼마 들었어?	
94	그게 옛날엔 먹혔어(=됐었어)? 이젠 쉽지 않지.	
95	그게 예전엔 너의 꿈이었어?	
96	이거 예전엔 공짜였어? 좋았네.	
97	옛날엔 5%였어? 지금은 10%인데.	
98	가격이 예전엔 더 낮았어?	더 낮은 lower
99	이거 예전엔 느렸어? 상상할 수가 없다.	느린 slow
100	그거 예전엔 어디에 있었어?	

복습강의 MP3

Positive (긍정)	Negative (부정)	Question (의문)
Do/Go …. [동사 바로]	Don't	-
해, 하세요	하지 마, 하지 마세요	-
I used to	I didn't use to	Did you use to?
옛날엔 했었는데… (지금은 안 해)	옛날엔 안 했었는데… (지금은 해)	옛날엔 했었어?

01	나 울 것 같아. 이별하는 건 힘들어. [이별하다 say goodbye]
02	울고 싶다. 모든 게 엉망이야. [엉망 a mess]
03	나 지금 당장 울 수 있어. 내기 할래? [내기하다 bet]
04	울고 싶었는데, 못 울었어.
05	저 애 우는데. 저 애랑 얘기 좀 해봐.
06	나도 울지도 몰라. 그만 울어. [그만하다 stop -ing]
07	그 앤 많이 울어. 울보야. [울보 a crybaby]
08	너 떠났을 때, 나 많이 울었어. 아기처럼 울었어. [처럼 like]
09	울지 마. 나도 울 거야.
10	그만 울게.
11	내가 그 애 봤을 때, 울고 있었어.
12	나라도 울겠어. 가끔은, 우는 게 도움이 돼. [우는 것 crying]
13	울고 싶으면, 울어. 울고 나면, 기분 나을 거야.
14	그 앤 예전에 많이 울었었어. 예전엔 울보였어.
15	울음을 멈출 수가 없었어.

정답확인 : P 280

16	울고 싶지 않았는데… 너무 슬펐어.
17	난 회사에선 안 울 거야.
18	사람들 앞에서 울고 싶지 않아. [앞 in front of]
19	나 우는 거 아니야. 나 괜찮아.
20	난 회사에서 울지 않아.
21	회사에서 울어본 적 없어.
22	그 애만 빼고 모두다 울고 있었어. [빼고 except]
23	나 예전엔 별로 울지 않았는데.
24	난 지금 안 우는 게 좋겠어. (그건) 전문가 답지 않아. [전문가 다운 professional]
25	그 영화 슬펐는데, 난 울지 않았어.
26	그 앤 잘 안 울어.
27	왜 울어? 너 괜찮아?
28	왜 울었어? 무슨 일이(라도) 생겼니?
29	울고 싶어?
30	울 거야?

31	울고 있었어?
32	이미 지나간 일을 후회하고/울고 싶지 않아.
33	우리 이미 지나간 일에 후회하지 않는 게 좋을 것 같아.
34	전 이미 지나간 일은 후회하지 않아요.
35	나라면 이미 지나간 일을 후회하지 않겠어.
36	이제부터 난 이미 지나간 일을 후회하지 않을 거야. [이제부터 from now (on)]
37	내가 지금 이미 지나간 일을 후회하고 있는 건가?

추억

A: Can you turn it up? I want to listen to this song.

B: Ok. Is this good?

A: Yes, that's good. I used to love this song.

B: I like this song, too. I haven't heard it for a long time.

A: This used to be my favorite song. I used to listen to it over and over again.

B: It's over. Do you want to listen to something else?

A: I want to listen to it again. Could/Can/Would you play the song again?

B: Yes, I will play it again.

A: This song brings back some memories.

B: You are right. Songs do that.

A: I used to listen to it when I was a university student.

I used to sing this song when I went to karaoke with my friends.

This used to be my go-to-karaoke song.

What were you doing when you were listening to this song?

B: This song reminds me of my ex-girlfriend.

This song was popular when I was with her.

We broke up and it was very hard. I used to cry when I

was listening to this song.

A: Did you really cry? It's hard to believe.

B: I used to be romantic.

추억

A: 소리 좀 키워줄래? 이 노래 듣고 싶어.

B: 알았어. 이 정도 좋아?

A: 응, 그거 좋네. 나 예전에 이 노래 좋아했었어.

B: 나도 이 노래 좋아해. 이거 안 들어본 지 오래됐다.

A: 이게 내가 예전에 가장 좋아하는 노래였어. 예전에 이 노래

계속 들었었어. [계속 over and over again]

B: 끝났네. [끝난 over] 다른 거 들을래?

A: 그 노래 또 듣고 싶어. 그 노래 다시 틀어 줄래? [틀다 play]

B: 그래, 또 틀게.

A: 이 노래가 기억을 가져온다. (=예전 생각이 난다) [가져오다

bring back]

B: 네 말이 맞아. 노래들이 그렇지. (=노래가 그렇게 하지)

A: 내가 대학생때 이 노래를 들었었어.

친구들 이랑 노래방에 가면 이 노래 불렀었지.

이게 예전에 내 18번이였어. [18번 one's go-to-karaoke song]

넌 이 노래 들을 때, 뭐 하고 있었어?

B: 이 노래는 내 전 여자친구를 생각나게 하네. [생각나게 하다, 상

기시키다 remind-of]

내가 그녀 랑 있을 때, 이 노래가 인기가 많았어.

우린 헤어졌고, 참 힘들었어. 이 노래 들을 때, 많이 울곤 했어.

A: 너가 정말 울었어? 믿기 힘든데.

B: 나 예전에 로맨틱 했거든.

만남

A: It's so good to see you! I haven't seen you for ages.

B: That's true. How long has it been?

A: It's been 10 years or so.

B: When did we last see each other?

A: We last saw each other at Jim's wedding.

B: That's right. I remember. Has it really been 10 years? Wow… Time flies.

A: How have you been?

B: Same old, same old. How about you? How have you been?

A: I have been good. How's your wife? Is she well?

B: Yes, she's good. Thank you for asking.

A: We used to be very close. We used to hang out all the time. I miss those days.

B: Yeah, we used to have a lot of fun together. Do you have kids/children?

A: Yes, I have a daughter and a son.

B: How old are they?

A: My daughter is 12 and my son is 8. Are you seeing someone/anyone?

B: Yes, I am seeing someone. We are going to get married next year.

A: Wow, that's good news.

_____

만남

A: 너 봐서 너무 좋다! 너 안 본지 정말 오래 됐어. [정말 오래 for ages]

B: 그게 사실이지. (=맞아) 얼마나 오래 됐지?

A: 10년 정도 됐어. [10년 쯤돼 10 years or so]

B: 우리 서로 언제 마지막으로 봤더라?

A: 우리 서로 Jim의 결혼식에서 마지막으로 봤지.

B: 맞아. 기억 난다. 정말 10년 된거야? 시간 빠르다. (=시간이 날아간다)

A: 어떻게 지냈어?

B: 똑같지 뭐. [Same old, same old] 넌? 넌 어떻게 지냈어?

A: 난 잘 지냈어. 와이프는 어때? 잘 지내?

B: 어 잘 지내. 물어봐 줘서 고마워.

A: 우리 예전에 매우 가까웠는데. 우리 항상 어울렸잖아. [어울리다 hang out 항상 all the time] 그때가 그립다. [그때 those days]

B: 그래, 우리 예전에 같이 재미있는 시간 보냈었는데. 아이들 있니?

A: 딸 하고, 아들 있어.

B: 몇 살이야?

A: 딸은 12살이고, 아들은 8살이야. 넌 누군가 만나니? [만나다,

연애하다 see]

B: 어, 누군가 만나고 있어. 우리 내년에 결혼할 거야.

A: 와, 좋은 소식이다.

Unit

3

과거 속 미래 의도를 말하고 싶을 때

'하려고 했었는데… (안 했어)' was going to

'be going to'의 과거형태인 'was/were going to'는 과거에서의 미래계획을 나타낼 수 있어요. 현재 결과와 상반되는 본래의 의도를 설명해 줄 수 있는 유용하고 활용도 높은 표현입니다.

Positive (긍정)	Negative (부정)	Question (의문)
I He She It was going to (was gonna)	I He She It wasn't going to (wasn't gonna)	Was I he she it going to? (gonna)?
You We They were going to (were gonna)	You We They weren't going to (weren't gonna)	Were you we they going to? (gonna)
하려고 했었는데… (안 했어)	안 하려고 했었는데… (했어)	하려고 했었어?

해설강의 MP3

이렇게 만듭니다!

문장의 핵심단어인 '동사'를 넣습니다!

Positive (긍정)	Negative (부정)	Question (의문)
나 이거 사려고 했었는데…	이거 안 사려고 했었는데…	뭐 사려고 했었어?
(안 샀어)	(샀어)	
I was going to buy it.	I wasn't going to buy it.	What were you going to buy?

긍정문 I was going to

☞ 오른쪽 힌트를 이용해서, 직접 문장을 만들어보세요!

훈련용 MP3

정답확인 : P 281

01	내가 그거 하려고 했었는데… 미안.	
02	내가 너한테 전화 하려고 했었는데, 깜빡했어.	
03	어제 숙제 하려고 했었는데. 시간이 없었어.	
04	그 애가 너한테 알려주려고 했었는데.	
05	내가 그 애한테 먼저 물어보려고 했었는데. 기회가 없었어.	
06	오늘 집 청소하고, 요리도 하려고 했었는데. 하루 종일 밖에 있었어. 아무것도 할 힘(에너지)이 없어.	
07	너가 왔을 때, 막 샤워하려고 했었어.	
08	우리 지금 막 나가려던 중이었어.	
09	오늘 아침에 늦잠 자려고 했었는데. 너가 날 깨웠어.	늦잠 자다 sleep in, 깨우다 wake-up
10	내가 널 위해 그거 사주려고 했었는데…	

11	나도 방금 그 말 하려고 했었는데…	
12	나 어차피 그거 너한테 주려고 했었어.	어차피 anyway
13	제가 그거 오늘 보내려고 했었는데요. 너무 늦었나요?	
14	그거 가져오려고 했었는데. 가져오는 거 깜빡했네.	
15	너 지금 뭔가 말 하려고 했었잖아. 먼저 해.	먼저 하다 go first
16	나 이거 해보려고 했었는데. 지금은 모르겠어.	
17	너 일찍 왔네. 내가 너 기다리려고 했었는데. 어떻게 이렇게 빨리 왔어?	이렇게 빨리 so fast
18	오늘밤에 이거 입으려고 했었는데. 크네. 살 빠졌어.	살 빠지다 lose weight
19	우린 그냥 집에 있으면서 TV 보려고 했었어.	
20	난 택시 타려고 했었지.	택시 타다 take a cab

긍정문 I was going to

☞ 오른쪽 힌트를 이용해서, 직접 문장을 만들어보세요!

21	내가 내려고 했었는데. 점심 고마워.	
22	여기서 좌회전 하려고 했었는데…	
23	난 이걸로 주문하려고 했었는데. 근데, 마음 **바꿨어.**	마음 바꾸다 change one's mind
24	**내가 먼저 사과하려고 했었는데… 이해해줘서 고마워.**	고마워 Thank you for
25	나도 이걸로 고르려고 했었는데. 너가 이거 원하면, **가져.**	
26	우리 막 저녁 먹으려고 했었어. 저녁 먹고 갈 수 있어?	
27	내가 그 앨 용서하려고 했었는데… 그 앤 정말 나빠. 그 앨 좋아하기 힘들어.	
28	**내가 그거 찾아 보려고(인터넷으로) 했었는데.** **나한테 말해줘서 고마워.**	(인터넷으로) 찾아 보다 look-up
29	그 애한테 화내려고 했었는데. 그 애의 귀여운 얼굴을 봐봐. 항상 내 분노를 녹여.	화내다 scold 녹다, 녹이다 melt 분노 anger
30	오늘부터 다이어트 하려고 했었는데… 이거 너무 맛있어 보여. 내일부터 시작하지 뭐.	다이어트 하다 go on a diet

31	내가 그 애 막으려고 했었는데. 그러고 싶었는데. 못 했어.	
32	나도 그거 무시하려고 했는데. 옛날엔 무시하는 거 쉬웠는데…	
33	난 그거 포기하려고 했었어. 하지만, 네가 날 많이 도와 줬어. 그건 절대 안 잊을거야.	
34	네가 도착하기 전에, 모든 걸 준비하려고 했었는데.	준비하다 prepare
35	우리 계약서에 싸인하려고 했었는데. 네가 망쳤어.	계약, 계약서 the contract 망치다 ruin
36	난 네 방식으로 하려고 했었지.	네 방식으로 your way
37	내가 그거 너한테 생일 선물로 주려고 했었는데. 뭐 갖고 싶어?	생일 선물로 as a birthday gift
38	거기 혼자 가려고 했었어. 아무도 가고 싶어하지 않더라고. 나랑 같이 가줘서 고마워.	
39	내가 너한테 어제 알려주려고 했었는데. 아직 결정 안 했어.	
40	우리 그거 취소하려고 했었는데. 그게 환불 불가였어.	환불 불가인 non refundable

부정문 I wasn't going to

☞ 오른쪽 힌트를 이용해서, 직접 문장을 만들어보세요!

41	어젯밤에 안 나가려고 했었는데. 어디 가야 했어.	
42	나 이거 안 먹으려고 했었는데. 너무 맛있었어.	
43	안 울려고 했었는데. 너무 감동적이었어.	감동적인 moving / touching
44	아무말도 안 하려고 했었는데. 너무 화가 났었어.	너무 화난 furious
45	널 귀찮게 하지 않으려고 했는데⋯ 미안. 이게 마지막이야.	마지막 the last time
46	아무것도 안 사려고 했었는데⋯ 많은 것을 샀어. 돈 많이 썼네.	(돈) 쓰다 spend
47	나 여기 다시는 안 오려고 했었는데.	
48	거짓말 안 하려고 했었는데⋯ 선택의 여지가 없었어.	
49	그 애한테 말 안 하려고 했는데. 그 애가 계속 물어봤어.	계속하다 keep -ing
50	내가 이 말은 안 하려고 했었는데⋯ 그 앤 좋은 사람이 아니야.	

51	포기 안 하려고 했었는데… 계속 할 수가 없었어.	계속 하다 continue / keep going
52	나 그거 버리려고 한 건 아니었는데. 실수였어.	
53	돈 인출 안 하려고 했었는데… 현금만 되더라고.	인출하다 withdraw 현금만 되는 cash only
54	이번엔 스케줄 재조정 안 하려고 했었는데. 죄송합니다.	
55	그거 더 이상 생각 안 하려고 했었는데. 그 생각하는 걸 멈출 수가 없어.	멈추다 stop-ing
56	그 앤 나랑 말(이야기) 안 하려고 했었어. 근데, 결국엔 우리 화해했어.	결국엔, 결국은 eventually 화해하다 make up
57	정크푸드 안 먹으려고 했었는데. 정크푸드 맛 너무 좋아.	정크푸드 junk food 맛이 나다 taste
58	난 그 애 다신 안 보려고 했었어. 하지만, 그 애 많이 변했어. 너가 그 애 보면, 너도 놀랄거야.	
59	그거 녹음 안 하려고 했었는데. 다 녹음했어. 여기 있어.	녹음/녹화하다 record
60	무리하지 않으려고 했었는데… 난 뭔가 시작하면, 멈추기가 힘들어.	무리하다 overdo

부정문 I wasn't going to

☞ 오른쪽 힌트를 이용해서, 직접 문장을 만들어보세요!

61	나 그거 삭제 안 하려고 했었는데. 이거 복구할 수 있나요?	복구하다 restore
62	내 시간 낭비 하지 않으려고 했는데. 오늘 시간 많이 낭비했어.	낭비하다 waste
63	밀당 안 하려고 했었는데… 너가 먼저 시작했잖아.	밀당하다 play hard to get/play a game with
64	미안. 안 웃으려고 했었는데. 나 너 비웃는거 아니야. 그냥 웃는 거지. 알았어. 이제 그만 할게.	비웃다 laugh at
65	이번 여름엔 아무데도 안 가려고 했었는데.	
66	노래 안 하려고 했었는데. 모두가 원하니까. 노래 딱 한 곡 부를게요.	하니까, 때문에, 하므로 since
67	아무것도 기대 안 하려고 했었는데…	
68	그 애랑 안 싸우려고 했었는데. 난 정말 노력했는데.	노력하다 try
69	화 안 내려고 했었는데… 하지만 서비스가 엉망이었어.(=나빴어)	화내다 get angry 엉망인 terrible/awful
70	내 약속 안 깨려고 했었는데. 정말 미안해.	약속 깨다 break one's promise

의문문 Were you going to?
☞ 오른쪽 힌트를 이용해서, 직접 문장을 만들어보세요!

71	넌 거기서 뭐 하려고 했었어?	
72	너 이걸로 뭐 하려고 했던 거야? 이게 왜 너의 주머니에 있어?	로,를 가지고 with
73	너 어딘가 가려던 거었어?	
74	어디 가려고 했었는데?	
75	언제 오려고 했었어? 오늘 오려고 했었니?	
76	너 뭔가 말하려던 거였어? 뭐라고 했어?	
77	그 애한테 어떻게 말하려고 했었어?	
78	너 어느 거 쓰려던 거였어? 이거 내가 써도 될까?	
79	뭐 사려고 했었는데?	
80	이거 어디다 두려고 했었어?	

의문문 Were you going to?

☞ 오른쪽 힌트를 이용해서, 직접 문장을 만들어보세요!

81	이거 언제 하려고 그런 거야?	
82	너 나한테 말 할 거였어? 언제 말 하려고 했었는데?	
83	그걸 나한테 어떻게 숨기려는 거였어? 웃기셔. 난 널 너무 잘 알아.	
84	이거 언제 고치려고 한거야?	
85	우리 어디 가려고 했던 거야? 알고 싶어.	
86	날 어디 데려가려고 했었는데?	데려가다 take
87	거기 얼마나 오래 있으려고 했었어? 너의 원래 계획이 뭐였어?	원래 계획 original plan
88	이걸 혼자서 하려고 했던 거야? (너에게) 내가 있잖아.	혼자서, 스스로 by oneself
89	나 없이 어떻게 살아 남으려고 했었어? 당신은 내가 필요해. 나 없이 살 수 있어?	살아 남다 survive
90	이거 반품하려고 했었어? 내가 이거 열었는데…	반품하다 return

의문문 Were you going to?

☞ 오른쪽 힌트를 이용해서, 직접 문장을 만들어보세요!

91	혼자 가려고 했었어? 너가 원하면, 내가 같이 갈 수 있어.	
92	**거기 차로 가려고 했었어 아님 기차 타려고 했었어?**	차로 가다 drvie
93	이거 언제 시작하려고 했어? 내가 너라면, 지금 당장 시작할 거야.	
94	**"Yes"라고 말하려고 했지? 너 "yes"라고 말했다.**	
95	언제 결정하려고 했어? 마음 정했니?	마음 정하다 make up one's mind
96	**이 책 읽으려고 했었니?**	
97	나한테 뭐 말하려던 거였어? 지금 말해줘. 난 들을 준비 되어 있어. (=난 '다 귀'야.)	들을 준비 되어 있는 = 다 귀인 all ears
98	**이거 장바구니에 넣으려고 했어?**	장바구니에 넣다 add-to cart
99	미안. 이거 쓰려고 하던 거였어요? 여기요.	
100	**우리 사장님도 초대하려고 했었어? 나라면 초대 안 해. 초대하지 말아줘.**	사장님 boss

복습강의 MP3

Positive (긍정)	Negative (부정)	Question (의문)
Do/Go …. [동사 바로]	Don't	-
해, 하세요	하지 마, 하지 마세요	-
I used to	I didn't use to	Did you use to?
옛날엔 했었는데… (지금은 안 해)	옛날엔 안 했었는데… (지금은 해)	옛날엔 했었어?
I was going to	I wasn't going to	Were you going to?
하려고 했었는데… (안 했어)	안 하려고 했었는데… (했어)	하려고 했었어?

01	내게 아무거나 물어봐. 난 준비됐어.
02	나 그 애한테 뭔가 물어보고 싶어.
03	내가 그 애한테 부탁할게.
04	나 너한테 뭔가 물어봐야 돼.
05	우리 그 애한테 먼저 물어보는게 좋을 것 같아.
06	그 애가 너한테 부탁할 것 같아.
07	내가 너한테 개인적인 질문할 건데, 나한테 대답해줘야 돼.
08	부탁하기가 어려웠어.
09	내가 너한테 부탁하잖아. 날 위해 해줄 수 있어?
10	나 너한테 뭔가 물어보고 싶었는데. 까먹었다.
11	내가 그 애한테 부탁했어. 그 애가 도와줄 거야.
12	그 앤 너무 많은 질문을 해. [너무 많은 질문 too many questions]
13	얘가 어렸을 땐, 많은 질문을 했었어.
14	나도 그거 너한테 물어보려고 했었는데.
15	인터뷰에서 그들이 개인적인 질문을 할지도 몰라.

정답확인 : P 286

16	나라면 도움을 요청할 거야. [도움 요청하다 ask for help]
17	매번 나한테 물어보지 않아도 돼. [매번 every time]
18	그 애한테 더 이상 부탁할 수 없어. 너무 많이 부탁했어. [너무 많이 too many times]
19	그 애한테 물어보기 싫어. 그 앤 친절하지 않아.
20	나 너한테 부탁하지 않았잖아. 너가 그냥 한 거지.
21	묻지 마. 더 이상 생각하고 싶지 않아.
22	인터뷰에서 그들이 내게 많은 질문을 하지 않았어. 나쁜 징조 인가? [나쁜 징조 a bad sign]
23	난 질문하지 않아. [질문하다 ask questions] 난 그냥 하지.
24	난 질문하지 않아도 돼. 그 애 그냥 모든 걸 내게 말해줘.
25	그 애한테 아직 물어보지 않았어. 내가 그애 볼 때, 할 게.
26	그 애한테 못 물어봤어. 난 그 애랑 이야기할 기회가 없었어.
27	그 애한테 부탁하지 않을 거야. 어차피 '아니' 라고 할 것 같아. [어차피 anyway]
28	나이스하게 물어봐줄래? 내가 너라면, 난 나이스하게 부탁하겠어. [나이스하게 nicely]
29	나한테 뭐 물어보고 싶은데?
30	뭔가 물어봐도 되나요?

31	뭐 물어볼 거야?
32	뭐 물어보려고 했었어?
33	도움 요청했니?
34	내가 너무 많은 걸 요구하는 건가? [너무 많은 것 too much]
35	너가 나라면, 넌 뭘 물어보겠어?
36	내가 뭘 물어보는게 좋을 것 같아?
37	넌 뭘 물어볼 것 같아?
38	미안. 친구였어. 너 나한테 뭐 물어보고 있었지?
39	나 너한테 뭔가 물어볼 건데. 묻지도 말고 따지도 말고 해줄 수 있어?
40	난 묻지도 따지지도 않고 그거 했어.
41	이 제품이 맘에 안 들면, 묻지도 않고 따지지도 않고 반품할 수 있어요.
42	내가 묻지도 따지지도 않고 그거 할게.

일기 - 일과

I had so many things to do today. It was a long day.

I was going to call my parents and say hello to them, but I didn't. I was busy all day.

I met some friends of mine after (I finished) work. We had dinner together.

It was great to spend time with them. I had a good time.

-

I was going to go to the dentist this morning, but I had to cancel that.

We had to finish a project at work, so I was stuck in a meeting all morning.

We finished the project this afternoon. It was so good. I think it will be successful.

I did well today.

I love my job/work.

I am tired but I am happy.

I have many things to do tomorrow. Well, I like being busy.

I have to go to the dentist tomorrow morning. And I have to go to the gym after work.

I want to study English when I get home.

I am sleepy already. I am going to go to sleep/bed soon.

Dialogue Practice

일기 - 일과

오늘 할 일이 너무 많았다. 긴 하루였다.

부모님께 전화해서 인사하려고 했었는데, 안 했다. 하루 종일 바빴다.

퇴근 후에 친구들을 만났다. 우린 저녁을 같이 먹었다.

그들과 시간을 보내는 게 너무 좋았다. 좋은 시간을 보냈다.

-

오늘 아침에 치과에 가려고 했었는데, 취소해야 됐다.

우리가 회사에서 프로젝트를 마무리해야 돼서, 아침내내 회의에서 빠져나갈 수 없었다. [빠져나갈 수 없는, 갇힌 stuck in]

우린 오늘 오후에 그 프로젝트를 끝냈다. 너무 좋았다. 성공적일 것 같다.

난 오늘 잘 했다.

내 일을 사랑한다.

피곤하지만, 기분이 좋다.

내일 할 일이 많이 있다. 음, 난 바쁜 게 좋다.

내일 오전에 치과에 가야한다. 그리고 일이 끝난 후에 헬스장에

가야된다.

집에 오면 영어공부 하고 싶다.

벌써 졸리다. 금방 잘 거다.

일기 - 변화

I used to keep a diary.

I haven't written anything in my diary for a long time.

It's an excuse but I have been busy.

But I have decided to write something every day.

A lot of things have changed since I last wrote in the diary.

I used to work for a small company in Suwon. Now I work close to my place.

I didn't use to have much time for myself. I used to be tired all the time.

Now I have time to enjoy myself. I read, work out and study English.

It is fun to study English. I am proud of myself.

I used to bite my fingernails when I was anxious. I don't bite my fingernails now.

I used to complain a lot. And I used to be a little bit negative.

I am trying not to complain. I also try to see good in everything/all things.

Sometimes, bad things happen in life. We can't avoid them.

They are unwanted things, but they may not be terrible things.

A crisis can be/become an opportunity. No, crises are opportunities!

So, I try to see the good even in a bad situation.

I believe I can find positive sides/aspects in everything.

I have become a positive person. Am I getting on/old?

My relationship with my mother didn't use to be good. We used to fight a lot.

I have changed. It is nice to have a mother like my mom. I appreciate her.

일기 - 변화

예전엔 일기를 썼었다. [일기 쓰다 | keep a diary]

내 일기장에 아무것도 적지 않은 지 오래됐다.

핑계지만, 바빴다. [핑계 an excuse]

하지만, 매일 뭔가를 적기로 결심했다.

내가 마지막으로 일기에 쓴 이후로 많은 것들이 변했다.

예전에 수원에 있는 작은 회사에서 일을 했었다. 지금은 집에서

가까운 데서 일한다.

예전엔 날 위한 시간이 없었다. 항상 피곤해 했었다. [항상 all the

time]

지금은 내 자신을 즐길 시간이 있다. 독서, 운동하고 영어공부 한다.

영어 공부하는 게 너무 재미있다. 난 내 자신이 자랑스럽다.

예전엔 불안할 때 손톱을 물어 뜯었었다. 지금은 내 손톱 물어

뜯지 않는다. [불안한 anxious 물다 | bite]

예전엔 불평을 많이 했었다. 그리고, 조금은 부정적이었었다.

[부정적인 negative]

지금은 불평하지 않으려고 노력하고 있다. 난 또한, 모든 것 들

에서 좋음을 보려고 한다.

가끔은, 삶에 나쁜 일들도 생긴다. 우리는 그것들을 피할 수 없다.

그것들은 원치 않는 것들이지만, 끔찍한 일은 아닐지도 모른다.

[원치 않는 것들 unwanted things]

위기는 기회가 될 수 있다. [위기 a crisis 기회 an opportunity] 아니,

위기들은 기회다!

그래서, 난 나쁜 상황에서도 좋은 점을 보려고 한다.

모든 것 들에서 긍정적인 면을 찾을 수 있다고 믿는다.

난 긍정적인 사람이 되었다. 내가 늙어가고 있는 건가?

우리 엄마와의 관계가 예전엔 좋지 않았다. 우린 많이 싸웠었다.

난 변했다. 우리 엄마 같은 엄마가 있어서 너무 좋다. 감사하다.

[감사하다 appreciate]

Unit

4

무언가의 존재 여부를 말하고 싶을 때

'있어/있었어' There is & There was

한국말의 '있다/없다'에 해당하는 영어 표현 중, 무언가를 '소유'하는 것을 떠나서, 존재 여부를 나타낼 때 'there'를 사용해서 문장을 시작합니다.

예를 들어, 누군가의 소유가 아닌 공원이나, 산 과 바다, 혹은 특정 자리의 유무에 관해 이야기 할 수 있어서 역시 매우 많이 사용이 되는 표현입니다.

	Positive (긍정)	Negative (부정)	Question (의문)
현재	There is/are	There isn't/aren't	Is/Are there?
	있어	없어	있어
과거	There was/were	There wasn't/weren't	Was/Were there?
	있었어	없었어	있었어?

<주의>

There is/was 뒤에는 단수나 셀 수 없는 명사가 오고요,

There are/were 뒤에는 복수의 명사(보통 '-s'가 붙어요)가 옵니다.

이렇게 만듭니다!

존재하는 **무언가/누군가**를 나타내는 '**명사**'를 넣기만 하면 돼요!

	Positive (긍정)	Negative (부정)	Question (의문)
현재	문제가 있어. There is a problem. 사람 많아 (=많이 있어) There are many people.	문제 없어. There isn't a problem. 사람 많이 없어. There aren't many people	문제 있나요? Is there a problem? 사람 많아? Are there many people?
과거	문제 있었어. There was a problem. 사람 많았어. (=있었어) There were many people.	문제 없었어. There wasn't a problem. 사람 많이 없었어. There weren't many people	문제 있었니? Was there a problem? 사람 많았어? Were there many people?

have vs There is/are vs stay

have	가지고 있다, 소유하다 (주인공이 사람; 그 주인공이 가지거나 소유합니다)
There is/are	있다, 존재하다 (누구의 소유인지가 중요하지 않아요)
stay	있다, 머무르다

It vs There

It is It is enough. It is a problem.	'그것이~' 그거 = 충분해 그거 = 문제야
There is There is enough. There is a problem.	~가 '있다' 충분히 있어. 문제가 있어

긍정문 There is

☞ 오른쪽 힌트를 이용해서, 직접 문장을 만들어보세요!

훈련용 MP3

정답확인 : P 288

01	여기 안에 뭔가 있어.	
02	내 신발에 뭔가 있어.	
03	코너에 우체국이 있어.	코너에 on the corner
04	밖에 누군가 있어.	
05	차 앞에 누군가 있어.	
06	불이 켜져 있어.	불 켜있는 a light on
07	저희 호텔에는 수영장이 있어요. 연중 무휴 24시간 이용할 수 있어요.	연중 무휴 24시간 24/7
08	시간 충분히 있어.	
09	차 막혀.	차 막히는 a lot of traffic/ a traffic jam
10	이 국에 소금 너무 많아. 짜.	많은 소금 a lot of salt 짠 salty

긍정문 There is

☞ 오른쪽 힌트를 이용해서, 직접 문장을 만들어보세요!

11	기차가 10시에 있어.	
12	비행기가 오늘밤 11시에 있어.	
13	여기에 공항 (가는) 버스가 있어요.	공항으로 (가는) to the airport
14	문제가 있으면, 해결책도 있어.	해결책 a solution
15	가능성이 있어.	가능성 a possibility
16	길이 있어. (=방법이 있어.)	길, 방법 a way
17	이걸 해결할 방법 있어.	
18	할 말 (뭔가) 있어.	
19	내가 너한테 하고 싶은 말 (뭔가) 있어.	
20	너가 봐야 되는 게 (뭔가) 있어.	

긍정문 There are

☞ 오른쪽 힌트를 이용해서, 직접 문장을 만들어보세요!

21	사람이 너무 많아. (=많이 있어)	
22	차가 너무 많아.	
23	집에 방 3개 있어.	
24	그 반에 학생이 20명 있어.	
25	내 가족은 4명 있어.	명 people
26	테이블 위에 샌드위치가 좀 있어요. 드세요.	드세요. Help yourself.
27	항상 양면이 있잖아. 둘 다 들어봐야지.	양면 two sides 둘 다 both sides
28	좋은 책들이 많이있어. 어디서 시작할지 모르겠어요.	어디서 시작할지 where to begin
29	그런 경우가 있긴 한데요. (그건) 드물어요.	경우 case(s) 드문 rare
30	인생엔 많은 기복이 있지.	기복 ups and downs

31	생각해보면, 행복한 순간들이 많이 있어요. 인생 괜찮아요. 희망이 있어요. 🔊	행복한 순간들 happy moments 희망 a hope
32	많은 방법들이 있지. 🔊	많은 방법들 many ways
33	이거 할 방법 많아. (= 많이 있어) 🔊	
34	할 게 많아. (= 많은 것들이 있어) 나 오늘 너무 바쁘네. 🔊	많은 것들 many things
35	볼 거 많아. (=많은 것들이 있어) 🔊	
36	고를 게 너무 많아. 딱 한 개 고르기 어려워. 🔊	딱 하나 only one
37	할 말 많은데… 🔊	
38	하고 싶은 말 많아. 🔊	
39	우리가 할 수 있는 게 많아. 🔊	
40	나 오늘은 해야 되는 게 너무 많아. 🔊	

긍정문 There was/were

☞ 오른쪽 힌트를 이용해서, 직접 문장을 만들어보세요!

41	차가 막혔어. 여기 오는데 2시간 걸렸어.	
42	작은 문제가 있었지만, 내가 해결했어. 그거 이번 주말까지 다 될 거야.	
43	아무 대답이 없었어. (전화 안 받았어.)	아무 대답 없는 no answer
44	사고가 있었어.	사고 an accident
45	이유가 있었어. 왜냐고 묻지는 마.	이유 a reason 왜냐고 why
46	컨퍼런스가 대전에서 있었어. 그 컨퍼런스에 참석해야 됐어.	참석하다 attend
47	우리가 거기에 갔을 때, 긴 줄이 밖에 있었어. 오래 기다려야 됐어.	
48	그거 할 시간 충분히 있었어.	
49	그 반에 학생 많이 있었어.	
50	부재중 전화가 10통 있었어.	부재중 전화 missed calls

부정문 There isn't

☞ 오른쪽 힌트를 이용해서, 직접 문장을 만들어보세요!

51	그 안에 아무것도 없어.	
52	아무도 없는데. 모두 어디 있지?	
53	시간이 모자라. (= 충분히 없어)	
54	하나도 없어.	하나도 any
55	미안하지만, 커피가 하나도 안 남았어요. 차 마실래요?	남은 left
56	냉장고에 우유 없어. 우유 다 떨어졌어.	다 떨어지다 run out of
57	할 말이 (아무것도) 없다. 뭐라고 말할지 모르겠어.	
58	먹을 게 (아무것도) 없어.	
59	여긴 살 게 (아무것도) 없어.	
60	갈 데가 (아무데도) 없어.	

61	그 안에 아무것도 없었는데요.	
62	문제 없었어요. 네 덕분에, 성공적이었어.	덕분에 Thanks to 성공적인 succesful
63	나도 그거 하고 싶었는데, 시간이 충분히 없었어. 아마도 다음번에 (하자).	
64	문제 없었어.	문제 an issue
65	그런 옵션 없었어.	옵션 an option
66	자리가 모자랐어. (=충분히 없었어)	자리 room/space
67	여기에 아무도 없었어. 정말 외롭게 느껴졌었어.	
68	어제 지갑을 주웠는데, 그 안에 돈은 없었어.	줍다 find
69	그럴 기회가 없었어.	그럴 = 그렇게 할
70	어제 그 애 봤는데, 그 애랑 얘기할 기회는 없었어.	

부정문 There wasn't

☞ 오른쪽 힌트를 이용해서, 직접 문장을 만들어보세요!

71	입을 게 (아무것도) 없었어.	
72	할 게 (아무것도) 없었어. 너무 지루했어.	
73	배가 고팠는데, 먹을 게 (아무것도) 없었어.	
74	걱정할 거 (아무것도) 없었어.	
75	할 말이 (아무것도) 없더라고.	
76	널 대체할 사람은 (아무도) 없었어. 널 대체하기 힘들 거야.	대체하다 replace
77	얘기할 사람이 (아무도) 없었어.	
78	너무 늦었었어. 그래서, 먹을 데가 (아무데도) 없었어.	
79	내가 하고 싶었던 건 (아무것도) 없었어. 난 그냥 안에만 있고 싶었어.	
80	내가 필요했던 정보는 없었어. 시간 낭비 였어.	시간 낭비 a waste of time

의문문 Is/Are there?

☞ 오른쪽 힌트를 이용해서, 직접 문장을 만들어보세요!

81	이 근처에 은행 있나요?	이 근처 near/around here
82	사고가 났나?(=사고가 있나?) 차가 왜 이렇게 많이 있지?	
83	뜨거운 물 나와? (=뜨거운 물 있어?)	
84	상금이 있나요? 상금이 있으면, 나도 참여할래.	상금 a prize 참여하다 participate
85	그것에 대한 정보가 있나요? 어디서 찾을 수 있을까요?	
86	단 하나의 정답이 있는 건가요?	
87	집에 먹을 거 (뭔가) 있어? 집에 가기 전에, 뭔가 먹을까?	
88	갈 데 (어딘가) 있어요?	
89	제가 할 수 있는 게 (뭐라도) 있어요? 저 돕고 싶어요.	
90	자원봉사자 많이 있어요? 몇 명 있어요?	자원봉사자 volunteer(s)

의문문 Was/Were there?

☞ 오른쪽 힌트를 이용해서, 직접 문장을 만들어보세요!

91	실수가 있었나요? 제가 실수를 했나요? 죄송해요, 제가 수정할게요.	수정하다 correct
92	차 막혔어요?	
93	증인이 있었나요? 그걸 증명할 수 있나요?	증인 a witness 증명하다 prove
94	어젯밤에 정전 되었어?	정전 a blackout
95	이유가 있었니? (그) 이유가 뭐였어?	
96	배달에 문제가 있었나요?	배달 shipping/ delivery
97	얘기할 사람 (누군가) 있었어?	
98	네가 사고 싶은 게 (아무거라도) 있었어? 뭐라도 샀니?	
99	환자 많았어? 아픈 사람들 많았어?	환자 patient(s)
100	사람이 많았어요? 사람이 얼마나 많았어?	

Positive (긍정)	Negative (부정)	Question (의문)
Do/Go …. [동사 바로]	Don't	-
해, 하세요	하지 마, 하지 마세요	-
I used to	I didn't use to	Did you use to?
옛날엔 했었는데… (지금은 안 해)	옛날엔 안 했었는데… (지금은 해)	옛날엔 했었어?
I was going to	I wasn't going to	Were you going to?
하려고 했었는데… (안 했어)	안 하려고 했었는데… (했어)	하려고 했었어?
There is	There isn't	Is there?
있어	없어	있어?
There was	There wasn't	Was there?
있었어	없었어	있었어?

01	집에서 요리 할래. 저녁 먹고 가.
02	나 요리할 수 있어. 나 요리 잘해. [요리 잘하는 a good cook]
03	너가 요리하는 게 좋겠다. 난 요리 못해.
04	내가 그 앨 위해서 저녁 요리할 거야.
05	요리하기 쉬워.
06	지금 뭔가 요리하고 있는데. 5분 있다가 전화 다시 할게.
07	내가 널 위해서 요리할게.
08	그 애 요리 매일 해.
09	너가 왔을 때, 요리하고 있었어.
10	나 이거 요리 해봤어. 어떻게 하는건지 알아.
11	우리 같이 요리할지도 몰라.
12	우리 이거 집에서 요리하지 뭐.
13	내가 이거 어제 요리했어. 데울게. [데우다 heat-up]
14	내가 요리하려고 했었는데. 고마워.
15	엄마가 예전엔 매일 요리했었는데… 지금은 잘 안 하셔.

정답확인 : P 295

16	요리할 시간 있어. 5시 밖에 안 됐는데. [밖에 안 된 only]
17	요리하기 쉬웠어.
18	내가 요리하지 않는 게 좋겠어. 아무도 먹지 않을 거야.
19	요리하지 않아도 돼, 하고 싶지 않으면. 밖에 나가도 돼.
20	오늘밤은 요리하기 싫다. 뭔가 주문할까?
21	요리 못 했어. 시간이 없었어.
22	그 애 요리 안 해.
23	야채는 너무 오래 익히지 마세요. [오래 익히다 overcook]
24	내가 이거 너무 오래 익히려고 한 게 아니었는데…
25	내가 이거 요리하지 않았어. 샀어.
26	그 애 요리 해본 적 없어.
27	요리할 시간이 없었어.
28	요리할 게 아무것도 없어.
29	우리 뭐 요리할까?
30	우리 뭐 요리하는 게 좋을까?

31	뭐 요리했어?
32	뭐 요리할 거야?
33	오늘 저녁 요리 해줄래? 나 늦을 거야.
34	뭐 요리하고 싶어?
35	요리하세요? 이거 어떻게 요리하는지 아세요?
36	우리 어렸을 때, 엄마가 뭐 요리해줬었지?
37	무슨 요리하는 거야? 뭔가 냄새 좋다. [냄새 나다 smell]
38	내가 요리해야 돼? 내 차례야? [차례 one's turn]
39	요리할 시간이 있어?
40	그건 마치 첩첩산중 같다. [마치 ~같은 (just) like]
41	그건 마치 갈수록 태산 같았어.
42	난 더 나쁜 상황으로 들어갔어.

공항 체크인

A: Where are you flying to?

B: I am flying to New York.

A: Could I see your passport and ticket, please?

B: Certainly. Here you are.

A: Are you checking in any bags?

B: Yes, I'd like to check in two bags.

A: Did you pack your bags yourself?

B: Yes, I did. I packed them myself.

A: Are you carrying anything for anyone else?

B: No, I am not. I am not carrying anything for anybody else.

A: Place your bag on the scale, please.

B: Ok.

A: That's good. I will put this baggage tag for you. Can you put the second bag on the scale?

B: Yes, I can.

A: Do you prefer a window seat or an aisle seat?

B: Can I get a window seat, please?

A: Here is your boarding pass. Go through security, and your flight will depart from Gate 22. This is your seat number and this is your departure gate.

B: Thank you. What time do I have to board?

A: We will begin boarding at 9:20. Is there anything else you want to ask?

B: No, there isn't. Thank you so much.

A: You are all set. Enjoy your flight.

공항 체크인

A: 어디로 비행하세요?

B: 뉴욕으로 비행합니다.

A: 여권과 티켓을 봐도 되겠습니까?

B: 그럼요. 여기 있습니다.

A: 가방을 체크인 하시나요?

B: 네, 가방 두개를 체크인 하고 싶어요.

A: 가방을 직접 싸셨나요?

B: 네. 직접 쌌습니다.

A: 다른 사람을 위해 가지고 있는 게 있습니까? (=다른 누군가를 위해 아무것이라도 들고가는/나르는 것이 있나요?)

B: 아니요. 전 다른 사람을 위해 가지고 있는 게(=나르는 게) 아무것도 없습니다.

A: 저울 위에 가방을 놓아주세요.

B: 알겠습니다.

A: 좋아요. 당신을 위해 이 가방 표를 붙일게요. 두 번째 가방을 저울 위에 올려 주시겠어요?

B: 네.

A: 창가 석 혹은 복도 석 중 어느것을 선호하십니까?

B: 창가 석을 가질 수 있을까요?

A: 여기 당신의 탑승권이요. 보안검색 [security]을 통과하시고요, 당신의 항공편 [flight]은 22번 게이트에서 출발할 거예요. [출발하다] depart 이게 당신의 좌석 번호이고요, 이게 당신의 출발 게이트입니다.

B: 고마워요. 몇 시에 탑승해야 하나요?

A: 저희는 9시 20분에 탑승을 시작할 거예요. [시작하다] begin ~ing 물어보고 싶으신 게 (다른 거 아무거나) 있어요?

B: 아니요, 없습니다. 정말 감사합니다.

A: (당신은) 다 되었습니다. [다 된 all set] 즐거운 비행 되세요. (= 비행을 즐기세요)

공항 체크인

A: Hi. Where are you going today?

B: I am going to New York.

A: May I see your passport and booking confirmation, please?

B: Certainly. Here is my passport. I have a booking confirmation on my phone. I was going to print it out but I forgot. Is that alright?

A: Yes, that's alright. Could I see your phone?

B: Yes, I will get the booking details. Here is the booking confirmation.

A: Have you checked in online already?

B: Yes, I have. Could I change my seat? I have a middle seat. I would like an aisle seat if that's possible.

A: Let me check. You are lucky. There is one aisle seat left. I will change your seat now.

B: Thank you so much.

A: Do you have any suitcases to check in?

B: Yes, I have one suitcase to check in.

A: When did you pack your bag?

B: I packed my bag yesterday.

A: Did you pack the bag yourself?

B: Yes, I did.

A: Are there any electronic devices in the suitcase?

B: No, there aren't.

A: Could you put your suitcase on the scale, please?

B: Sure.

A: Do you need a paper copy of your boarding pass?

B: Yes, please. I think it will be better to have a paper copy of my/the boarding pass.

A: Ok. This is your boarding pass. Your flight leaves from Gate 19 and boarding begins at 11. Is there anything (else) I can help you with?

B: No, there's nothing (else). Thank you. Have a great day.

A: Have a good flight.

A: 안녕하세요. 오늘 어디로 가십니까?

B: 전 뉴욕으로 갑니다.

A: 여권과 예약 확인증 [booking confirmation] 을 볼 수 있을까요?

B: 네. [Certainly] 여기 제 여권이요. 전 휴대폰에 예약 정보를 가지고 있어요. 프린트를 하려고 했었는데, 잊었습니다. [프린트하다 print-out] 괜찮은가요? [괜찮은 alright]

A: 네, 괜찮습니다. 당신의 휴대폰을 봐도 될까요?

B: 네, 예약 상세 정보 [booking details] 를 가져올게요. 여기 예약 확인입니다.

A: 인터넷으로 이미 체크인을 하셨습니까?

B: 네, 했습니다. 제 좌석을 바꿀 수 있을 까요? 전 중간좌석을 가지고 있어요. 혹시 가능하다면, 복도석을 원합니다.

A: 확인해볼게요. 운이 좋네요. 하나의 복도석이 남아 있네요. 지금 당신의 좌석을 바꿀게요.

B: 정말 감사합니다.

A: 체크인 할 가방 [suitcase(s)] 있습니까?

B: 네, 체크인 할 가방이 하나 있습니다.

A: 언제 짐을 싸셨나요?

B: 어제 쌌습니다.

A: 짐을 직접 싸셨나요?

B: 네, 그렇습니다.

A: 가방안에 전자제품이 있습니까?

B: 없습니다.

A: 당신의 가방을 저울 위에 놓아주시겠습니까?

B: 물론이죠.

A: (당신의) 탑승권 종이로 [a paper copy] 필요하십니까?

B: 네. 탑승권 종이로 가지고 있는 게 더 나을 것 같습니다.

A: 알겠습니다. 이게 당신의 탑승권입니다. 당신의 항공편은 19번 게이트에서 출발하고, 탑승은 11시에 시작합니다. 제가 도와드릴 수 있는 게 (다른 아무것) 있나요?

B: 아니요. 아무것도 없습니다. 감사합니다. 좋은 하루 되세요.

A: 좋은 비행 되세요.

Unit

5

There has/have been & There will/might/used to be

존재 여부를 표현하는 'there'를 이용해서, 4단원에서 공부한 단순한 현재와 과거의 표현 이외에도 다양한 의미를 정교하게 표현해 낼 수 있어요. 현재완료(have p.p.)나 have to를 사용해서 다른 의미의 '현재'를 나타낼 수 있고, 미래 시제 와도 같이 사용할 수 있습니다.

Positive (긍정)	Negative (부정)	Question (의문)
There has/have been	There hasn't/haven't been	Has/Have there been?
있었어 (지금까지, 쭉)	없었어	있었어요?
There will be	There won't be	Will there be?
있을 걸, 있을 거야 (예측)	없을 걸, 없을 거야	있을까?
There is going to be	There isn't going to be	Is there going to be?
있을 거야 (계획 & 예측)	없을 거야	있을까?
There may/might be	There may/might not be	-
있을지도 몰라, 있을 수도 있어	없을지도 몰라, 없을 수도 있어	-
There used to be	There didn't use to be	Did there use to be?
옛날엔 있었어 (지금은 없어)	옛날엔 없었어 (지금은 있어)	옛날엔 있었어?
There has to be	There doesn't have to be	Does there have to be?
있어야 돼, 있어야 해	없어도 돼	있어야 돼?

이렇게 만듭니다!

그 존재하는 **무언가/누군가**를 나타내는 **'명사'**를 넣기만 하면 돼요!

Positive (긍정)	Negative (부정)	Question (의문)
시간 많이 있었어. There has been a lot of time.	시간이 없었어. There hasn't been any time.	시간 있었어? (지금까지) Has there been time?
시간 있을 거야. There will be time. There is going to be time.	시간 없을 거야. There won't be time. There isn't going to be time.	시간 있을까? Will there be time? Is there going to be time?
시간 있을지도 몰라. There may/might be time.	시간이 없을지도 몰라. There may/might not be time.	-
옛날엔 시간 있었는데. There used to be time.	옛날엔 시간 없었는데… There didn't use to be time.	예전엔 시간 있었어? Did there use to be time?
시간 있어야 돼. There has to be time.	시간 없어도 돼. There doesn't have to be time.	시간 있어야 돼? Does there have to be time?

will vs be going to

will	① 방금 결정한 것 ('할게') ② 예측 (개인적인 예측 : I think there will be) ③ 미래 사실
am, is, are going to	① 계획해 둔 것 ('할거야') ② 예측 (현 상황에 비춘 예측)

긍정문

☞ 오른쪽 힌트를 이용해서, 직접 문장을 만들어보세요!

훈련용 MP3

정답확인 : P 294

01	예전엔 사람이 많았었어. 사람들이 모든 곳에 있었어.	모든 곳 everywhere
02	사람 많을 거야.	
03	사람이 많을 수도 있어.	
04	연락할 사람이 (누군가) 있어야 되는데. 이분 혼자예요?	
05	우리 같은 사람이 많을지도 몰라.	같은, 처럼 like
06	그 애 같은 피해자들이 많을 거야.	피해자 victim(s)
07	차 막힐 것 같아. 우리 일찍 가는 게 좋겠어.	차 막히는 a lot of traffic/a traffic jam
08	차 막힐지도 몰라.	
09	여기 예전엔 차가 많이 막혔었어.	
10	내가 이 휴가에서 회사로 돌아가면, 이메일과 메세지들이 많이 있을 거야.	회사로 to work

긍정문

☞ 오른쪽 힌트를 이용해서, 직접 문장을 만들어보세요!

11	문제가 있을지도 몰라. 문제 있으면, 알려줘요.	
12	문제가 (계속) 많았어. 해결할 사람은 (아무도) 없고, 이건 정말 큰 문제야.	정말 큰 huge
13	예전엔 문제가 많았었는데…	
14	문제가 있을 것 같은데.	
15	이 문제에 대한 해결책이 있어야 돼.	해결책 a solution to
16	예전엔 자유시간이 많았는데. 좋았지.	자유시간 free time
17	시간 충분히 있을지도 몰라.	
18	화장실 갈 시간 있을 거예요.	
19	연설 후에 질문할 시간이 있을 거예요.	
20	우리 자신을 위한 시간이 있어야 돼.	

긍정문
☞ 오른쪽 힌트를 이용해서, 직접 문장을 만들어보세요!

21	내일 시험 볼지도 몰라. (=시험이 있을지도 몰라)	
22	다음주에 기말 시험이 있을 거예요.	기말 시험 final exams/tests
23	이번달엔 (계속) 시험이 너무 많았어.	
24	시험이 있어야 돼.	
25	또 다른 기회가 있을 거야. 괜찮아.	또 다른 another
26	또 다른 기회가 금방 있을 수도 있어. 누가 알아?	누가 알아? Who knows?
27	또 다른 기회가 있어야 되는데… 다음번엔 더 잘 할게.	
28	많은 기회들이 있을 거야.	
29	기회가 많았는데… 아직 늦지 않았어.	
30	다음 주말엔 세미나가 있을 지도 몰라요.	

31	변화가 많이 있었어. 모든 게 바뀌었네.	변화 change(s)
32	우리 학교에 변화가 있을 거예요. 새로운 선생님들이 있을 거예요. (새 선생님이 오실 거예요.)	
33	큰 변화가 있어야 해.	
34	우리 계획에 변화가 있을 수도 있어. 그런 일이 생기면, 알려줄게요.	
35	길이 있을 거야. 항상 길이 있어.	길, 방법 a way
36	방법이 있을 지도 몰라. 문 하나가 닫히면, 또 다른 문이 열려. 항상 그렇잖아.	그런 like that
37	방법이 있어야 되는데…	
38	더 나은 방법이 있을 것 같아.	
39	더 좋은 방법이 있어야 돼.	
40	그걸 해결할 방법 많이 있을 거야.	

긍정문

☞ 오른쪽 힌트를 이용해서, 직접 문장을 만들어보세요!

41	혜택이 많이 있을 거야.	혜택, 이로운 점 benefit(s)
42	혜택이 있어야지. 안 그러면, 무슨 소용이야?	무슨 소용이야? What's the point?
43	유혹이 많을 지도 몰라. 난 강해지고 싶어.	유혹 temptation(s)
44	유혹이 많이 있을 거야. 우리 강해져야 돼.	
45	너가 공항에 도착하면, 널 픽업할 누군가가 있을 거야.	
46	내일 저녁에 TV에서 축구 시합 있을 거야. 난 집에 일찍 가서 그거 보려고.	
47	새로운 기능들이 많이 있을 거예요.	기능 feature(s)
48	여기 예전엔 은행이 있었는데.	
49	여기에 새로운 상점들과, 빌딩이 생길 거야. (=있을 거야)	
50	장단점이 있을 거야. 우린 그 모든 장단점을 고려해보는 게 좋을 것 같아요.	장단점 pros and cons 고려하다 consider

긍정문

☞ 오른쪽 힌트를 이용해서, 직접 문장을 만들어보세요!

51	많은 재미있는 활동들이 있을 거야. 나라면 가고 싶을텐데.	활동들 activities
52	**먹을 거 많을 거야.** (=먹을 많은 것들이 있을 거야.)	많은 것들 many things
53	배울 게 많이 있을 거야. 우린 뭔가 새로운 걸 매일 배우잖아.	뭔가 새로운 것 something new
54	**할 거 많이 있을 것 같아. 재미있을 거야. 기대된다.**	
55	볼 거 많이 있을 거야.	
56	**갈데 많을 거야.** (=갈 많은 곳들이 있을 거야.)	많은 곳들 many places
57	모든 게 있을 거야. 아무것도 가져오지 않으셔도 됩니다.	
58	너가 필요한 모든 게 있을 거야.	
59	너가 필요한 게 (뭔가) 있을지도 몰라. 필요한 게 있으면, 언제든지 제게 오세요.	언제든지 any time
60	우리회사에 대해 불만 사항이 많이 있었어. 우린 새로운 아이디어가 필요합니다.	불평/불만 사항 complaint(s)

61	사람 많이 없을 거야.	
62	옛날엔 사람 많이 없었는데.	
63	사람 많이 없을지도 몰라.	
64	문제 없을 거야. 걱정할 필요 없어요.	
65	문제 없을지도 모르잖아.	
66	우리가 그 시스템 바꾼 이후로는, 문제가 없었어.	
67	모자랄 것 같아. (=충분히 없을 것 같아)	
68	모자랄 수도 있어. 더 가져가요 혹시 모르니까.	혹시 모르니까 just in case
69	또 다른 기회는 없을지도 몰라.	또 다른 another
70	똑같은 기회는 없을 거야. 하지만, 더 나은 기회가 있을 것 같아.	

부정문

☞ 오른쪽 힌트를 이용해서, 직접 문장을 만들어보세요!

71	아무 조건 없을 거야. 할래?	할래? Are you in?
72	이유 없어도 돼. 우리가 설명할 수 없는 것들이 있잖아.	것들 things
73	내일 할 일 많을 거 같아.	많은 것들 many things
74	걱정할 거 (아무것도) 없을 거야.	
75	집에 먹을 거 (아무것도) 없을지도 모르는데.	
76	그거 작은 마을인데. 갈데가 (아무데도) 없을 거야.	
77	할 말 (아무것도) 없을 거야.	
78	하고 싶은 말 (아무것도) 없을 거야.	
79	거기엔 내가 하고 싶은 거 (아무것도) 없을 거야. 난 가기 싫어.	
80	우리가 그 앨 위해서 할 수 있는 게 (아무것도) 없을지도 몰라.	

의문문
☞ 오른쪽 힌트를 이용해서, 직접 문장을 만들어보세요!

81	방법이 있을까요?	길, 방법 a way
82	해결책이 있을까요?	해결책 a solution
83	차 막힐까? 우리 언제 나가는 게 좋을까?	차 막히는 a lot of traffic/a traffic jam
84	사람 많을까? 어떻게 생각해?	
85	사람 얼마나 올까? (=몇 명 있을까?)	
86	옛날엔 여기 사람 많았어?	
87	이유가 있어야 돼? 이유 없는데.	
88	무료 wifi가 있을까요?	
89	문제가 있을까요?	
90	우리 사이에 미래가 있을까?	미래 a future 사이 between

의문문

☞ 오른쪽 힌트를 이용해서, 직접 문장을 만들어보세요!

91	시간이 있을까?	
92	박물관에 갈 시간이 있을까?	
93	시간 충분할까? (=충분히 있을까?)	
94	그걸 다 할 시간이 있을 것 같아?	
95	시간이 얼마나 있을까?	얼마의 시간 how much time
96	기회가 있을까요?	
97	이번 기회 놓쳤어. 또 다른 기회가 있을 것 같아?	놓치다 miss
98	식 후에 질문을 할 기회가 있을까요?	식 the ceremony
99	가능성이 있을까요?	가능성 a possibility
100	가능성이 얼마나 있을까요?	얼마의 가능성 how much possibility

복습강의 MP3

Positive (긍정)	Negative (부정)	Question (의문)
Do/Go …. [동사 바로]	**Don't**	-
해, 하세요	하지 마, 하지 마세요	-
I used to	**I didn't use to**	**Did you use to?**
옛날엔 했었는데… (지금은 안 해)	옛날엔 안 했었는데… (지금은 해)	옛날엔 했었어?
I was going to	**I wasn't going to**	**Were you going to?**
하려고 했었는데… (안 했어)	안 하려고 했었는데… (했어)	하려고 했었어?

Positive (긍정)	Negative (부정)	Question (의문)
There is	**There isn't**	**Is there?**
있어	없어	있어?
There was	**There wasn't**	**Was there?**
있었어	없었어	있었어?
There will be	**There won't be**	**Will there be?**
있을 거야	없을 거야	있을까?
There is going to be	**There isn't going to be**	**Is there going to be?**
있을 거야	없을 거야	있을까?
There has been	**There hasn't been**	**Has there been?**
있었어	없었어	있었어?
There may/might be	**There may/might not be**	-
있을 지도 몰라	없을 지도 몰라	-
There used to be	**There didn't use to be**	**Did there use to be?**
옛날엔 있었어	옛날엔 없었어	옛날엔 있었어?
There has to be	**There doesn't have to be**	**Does there have to be?**
있어야 돼	없어도 돼	있어야 돼?

01	난 너 보고 싶어.
02	너 이거 봐야 돼. 정말 재밌어. (웃겨)
03	이번 주말에 영화 볼 거야.
04	이번 금요일에 널 볼 수 있어.
05	다시 봐서 좋다. 잘 지냈니?
06	나 그 애 일주일에 한 번씩 봐.
07	나 그거 봤어.
08	나 그거 본적 있어.
09	나 그 애 이따 볼 수도 있어.
10	나 그거 여러 번 봤어.
11	우리 옛날엔 맨날 서로 봤었는데.
12	어제 그 애 보려고 했었는데, 그 애가 너무 바빴어. 그래서 그 애가 취소했어.
13	우리 이 영화 보지 뭐.
14	내가 보고 싶은 게 (뭔가) 있어.
15	볼 거 많을 거야. 재미있을 거야.

정답확인 : P 299

16	너 봐서 너무 좋았어.
17	난 그 애 다시 보고 싶지 않아.
18	난 그 애 다시 보지 않을 거야.
19	우리 더 이상 보지 않는 게 좋을 것 같아.
20	이번 주에는 너 못 보겠다.
21	너가 원하지 않으면, 안 볼게.
22	너 그 애 안 봐도 돼.
23	나 너 안 본지 오래됐어. 어떻게 지냈어?
24	나 그 애 잘 안 봐.
25	나 아직 그거 안 봤어. 나중에 볼 거야.
26	나 어제 그 애 안 봤어.
27	내가 너라면, 난 이 영화 안 볼 거야.
28	이거 너 없이 안 보려고 했었는데. 할 게 (아무것도) 없었어. 너무 지루했어.
29	나 거기 갔을 때, 그거 못 봤어. 없던데.
30	그 애 우리 안 볼지도 몰라.

31	내가 봐도 될까?
32	뭐 볼 거야?
33	뭐 볼래?
34	우리 뭐 볼까?
35	우리 뭐 보는게 좋을까?
36	뭐 봤어?
37	이 영화 봤니?
38	뭐 보려고 했었는데?
39	보고 싶은 거 (아무거나) 있어?
40	볼 거 많을까?
41	볼 거 많았어?
42	우리는 의견이 같았어. 우린 항상 의견이 같아.
43	우리는 의견이 같지 않았어.
44	엄마는 나와 의견이 같지 않아.

A: Hi, where are you flying to?

B: I am flying to LA.

A: May I see your passport and ticket, please?

B: Sorry. They are in my bag. I will get them (out).

A: Which seat do you prefer? A window seat or an aisle seat?

B: I prefer a window seat.

A: I'm sorry. There aren't any window seats left. We have middle seats and aisle seats.

B: Can I get an aisle seat?

A: Yes, you can. How many suitcases do you want to check in?

B: I only/just have a carry on.

A: Ok. I will give you a baggage tag. You have to put this tag on it.

B: Thank you.

A: Do you have any liquids in your bag? You can't take any liquids on the plane.

B: I don't have any liquids in the bag.

A : Your flight has been cancelled due to bad weather.

B : Oh. I was worried about that. When is the next available flight?

A : It is tomorrow morning.

B : Ok. There is no choice.

A : Here is the printed confirmation. I'm sorry for the trouble.

B : That's ok. It's not your fault. Are there any hotels near the airport?

A : Yes, there are. You can get the information about hotels at the customer service desk. And if you go to the customer service desk, you can get/claim a voucher for hotels and meals.

B : Thank you. Where is the customer service desk?

A : It's on the second floor.

B : Thank you for your help.

A : My pleasure.

A: 안녕하세요. 어디로 비행하세요?

B: LA로 비행합니다.

A: 여권과 티켓을 봐도 되겠습니까?

B: 죄송해요. 가방에 있어요. 꺼낼게요.

A: 어느 좌석을 선호하세요? 창가 석 아니면 복도 석?

B: 창가석을 선호합니다.

A: 죄송합니다. 창가 석 남은 게 없습니다. 저희는 중간과 복도 석이 있네요.

B: 복도석으로 할 수 있을까요?

A: 네, 그렇게 해도 됩니다. 몇 개의 가방을 체크인 하실래요?

B: 전 기내 수화물 만 있습니다. [기내 수화물 carry on]

A: 알겠습니다. 가방 표[baggage tag]를 하나 드릴게요. 이 표를 그 위에 붙여야 해요.

B: 감사합니다.

A: 가방에 액체[liquid] 가지고 있습니까? 액체는 비행기로 가져갈 수 없습니다.

B: 전 가방에 액체를 가지고 있지 않습니다.

A: 당신의 비행이 나쁜 날씨로 취소가 되었습니다. [Your flight has been cancelled due to bad weather.]

B: 아, 그게 걱정이 되었습니다. 다음 이용 가능한 비행은 언제 입니까?

A: 내일 아침입니다.

B: 알겠습니다. 선택의 여지가 없네요. [선택의 여지 no choice]

A: 여기 확인서입니다. [확인서 printed confirmation] 죄송합니다. [I'm sorry for the trouble.]

B: 괜찮습니다. 당신의 잘못이 아니에요. 공항 근처에 호텔들 이 있나요?

A: 네, 있습니다. 고객서비스 데스크에서 호텔에 관한 정보를 얻을 수 있어요. 그리고, 고객서비스 센터에 가시면, 호텔과 음식을 위한 바우처를 받을 수 있습니다.

B: 감사합니다. 고객 서비스 데스크는 어디에 있나요?

A: 2층에 있습니다.

B: 당신의 도움 감사합니다.

A: 천만에요. [My pleasure.]

공항 체크인

A: How many suitcases would you like to check in?

B: I would like to check in one suitcase.

A: Did you pack it yourself?

B: Yes, I did.

A: Have you left your bag unattended at any time?

B: I'm sorry. What do you mean?

A: Has it been with you since you packed it? Have you left your bag alone?

B: No, I haven't left it alone. It has been with me since I packed it.

A: Has anyone given you anything to carry on the flight?

B: No.

A: Could you place your suitcase on the scale?

B: Yes. It's quite heavy.

A: I'm sorry but this suitcase is overweight. The limit is 20 kilos.

B: What should I do?

A: You have to take some things out if you don't want to pay for the excess. Or you can pay for an/the excess baggage charge.

B: How much will that be?

A: It's 90 dollars for a bag up to 30 kilos.

B: I will take some things out.

공항 체크인

A: 몇 개의 가방을 체크인 하실래요?

B: 이 가방 하나를 체크인 하고 싶어요.

A: 직접 싸셨습니까?

B: 네, 그렇습니다.

A: 언제라도 당신의 가방을 혼자 (내버려) 둔 적이 있습니까?

[혼자 unattended 언제(라)도 at any time]

B: 죄송합니다. 무슨 말(=의미)입니까?

A: 가방을 싼 후로 (그게) 항상 당신과 있었습니까? 가방을 혼
자 둔 적 있어요? [혼자 alone]

B: 아니요. 혼자 둔 적 없습니다. 가방 싼 이후로 저와 쭉 있었
습니다.

A: 누구라도 당신에게 비행기로 가져가라고 (아무것이라도) 준
적 있나요?

B: 아니요.

A: 가방을 저울에 올려 주시겠습니까?

B: 네. 꽤 무거워요.

A: 죄송하지만, 이 가방은 무게 초과네요. [무게 초과 overweight]
제한은 20 킬로입니다.

B: 어떻게 하지요? (=뭘 하는게 좋을까요)

A: 초과 분[the excess]을 내고 싶지 않으시면, 물건을 좀 빼야 합니다. [빼다 take-out 물건 some things] 아니면 초과 가방 요금을 내셔도 됩니다. [초과 가방 요금 an/the excess baggage charge]

B: 그게 얼마일까요?

A: 30킬로까지 가방 한 개에 90불입니다. [(상한)까지 up to]

B: 물건을 좀 뺄게요.

Unit

6

간접의문1 - 일반동사

여러 의미를 말할 때, 보통 문장(주어 와 동사)을 새로 시작해서 말하지만, 한 문장 안에 두 개의 동사가 어우러진 복잡한 표현들도 많아요.

특히 의문문 문장(예: 뭐 하고 싶어?)을 다른 문장(예: 말해줄래?) 속에 넣어서 표현하면(예: 뭐하고 싶은지 말해줄래?), 정말 다양한 말을 할 수 있게 됩니다.

Indirect questions

I know
I have to know
I want to know
I don't know
I forgot
I don't/can't remember
Tell me
Do you know
Can you tell me

what you want.
의문사 + 주어 + 동사

문장을 매끄럽게 연결하기 위해서, 의문 형태의 문장이 그 의미 그대로인 '긍정'이나 '부정'의 형태로 들어가게 됩니다.

원래 말하고 싶은 문장 바로 뒤에 의문사 + 주어 + 동사 를 넣어요.

제가 어떻게 도울 수 있는지 알고 싶어요.
I want to know how I can help.

이거 어디서 샀는지 말해줄래요?
Can you tell me where you bought it?

<주의>

'의문사'가 없다면 **'if/whether'**(혹시/그런지 아닌지)를 넣어야 돼요!

제가 도울 수 있는지 알고 싶어요.
I want to know if I can help.

내가 그걸 샀는지 기억이 안 나.
I can't remember whether I bought it (or not).

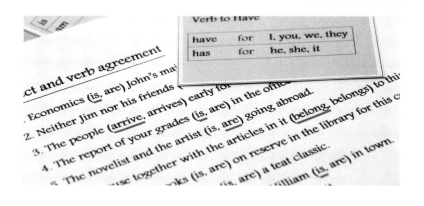

정답확인 : P 301

01	너 지금 어디 가야 되는지 말해줄래? 어디 가는 거야?	
02	넌 어디 가고 싶은지 말해봐. 너가 어디 가고 싶어하는지 알고 싶어.	
03	우리 이번 여름엔 어디 갈지 모르겠어. 제주도 갈지도 몰라.	
04	난 이번엔 어디로 가는 게 좋을지 모르겠어. 중국 아직 안 가봤는데. 너 거기 가봤니?	
05	언제 갈 수 있는지 확실하지 않아. 아직도 회사야. 할 게 많아.	할 게 많아. = 할 많은 것들 이 있어/가지고 있어.
06	너 지금 어디 가는지 알고 싶어.	
07	어제 너 어디 갔었는지 말해줘.	
08	그 애 어디 갔는지 모르겠어. 어디 갔지?	
09	그 애 어디 가고 있었는지 궁금하네.	
10	언제 가도 되는 건지 물어봐야겠다.	

11	내가 뭘 하고 싶은지 모르겠어. 내가 뭘 원하는지 그리고, 뭘 할 수 있는지 알고 싶어.	
12	우리 이젠 뭘 해야 하는지 넌 알아? 우리 이제 뭐 하지?	
13	내가 널 위해서 뭘 할 수 있는지 알고 싶어. 내가 널 얼마나 지지하는지 알잖아.	얼마나 how much 지지하다 support
14	너가 뭘 하는 게 좋을지 난 알아. 밖에 더 나가는 게 좋겠어. 너 그렇게 하면, 기분이 더 나을 거야.	
15	내일 뭐 할건지 확실하지 않아. 아무 계획(약속) 없어. 넌 뭐 할건데?	약속, 계획 plan(s)
16	내가 지금 뭐 하고 있는지 모르겠네. 이게 누굴 위한 거지? 날 위한 건가?	
17	어제 뭐 했는지 기억이 안 나. 어제 별 거 안 했어.	별 거, 별로 much
18	그 애 뭐 하는지 (원래) 아니? 회계사야.	회계사 an accountant
19	지금까지 뭐 했는지 보여줄래요?	지금까지 so far
20	그 애 거기서 뭐 하고 있었는지 궁금하네. 그 애 거기 안 가는데.	

21	너 뭐가 필요한지 알고 싶어.	
22	내가 뭐가 필요할지 모르겠어.	
23	그 애가 뭘 원하는지 넌 알아?	
24	그 애가 왜 이해를 못 하는지 궁금해.	
25	뭐 먹고 싶은지 모르겠어.	
26	그 애가 뭔가 말했는데. 그 애가 뭐라고 말했는지 까먹었어.	
27	너 어디 갈건지, 누구랑 갈 건지, 그리고 거기 얼마나 오래 있을 건지 말해줄래?	
28	이거 언제 배달해 줄 수 있는지 알려줄래요?	
29	내가 뭘 잘못한 건지 모르겠어. 난 아무것도 잘못하지 않았어.	잘못 하다 do wrong
30	저 어느걸로 써야 되는지 모르겠어요. 어느걸로 쓰는 게 좋은지 말해줄래요?	

31	너 몇 시에 올 수 있는지 알려줄래?	
32	제가 몇 시에 와야 되는지 알아요?	
33	몇 시에 **퇴근**인지 말해줄래요?	퇴근하다 = 일 끝나다
34	내가 얼마나 노력을 했는지 넌 몰라. 넌 절대 모를 걸.	얼마나 열심히 how hard 노력하다 try
35	그 애가 뭐라고 할지 모르겠어.	
36	**무슨말인지 알아요.** (=너의 의미가 뭔지 알아.)	뜻하다, 의미하다 mean
37	이게 무슨 뜻인지 아니?	
38	너 한국 **온지** (=있은지) 얼마나 오래 됐는지 알고 싶어.	
39	너가 뭐라고 말하려고 했는지 난 알아. 말 안 해도 돼.	
40	우리 어디서 만날 건지 확실하지 않아.	

41	이게 몇 시에 시작할지 모르겠어요. 금방 시작해야 되는데.	
42	그 애 어디 사는지 알아? 이 근처 살아?	
43	내가 집에 몇 시에 왔는지 궁금하네.	
44	내가 널 어떻게 도울 수 있는지 알고 싶어.	
45	여기에 뭘 써야 하는지 말해줄래요?	
46	너 그 애 왜 싫어하는지 이해가 안 돼. 그 애 정말 괜찮은데.	
47	너 어디에서 머물고 있는지 알고 싶어.	
48	너 그걸로 뭘 하려고 했었는지 모르겠어.	
49	내가 어디에 주차했는지 생각이 안 나.	
50	우리 뭐 살 건지 알아야지.	

51	내가 그 앨 왜 이해해야 되는지 이해가 안 돼.	
52	뭐 갖고 싶은지 말해줘.	
53	이게 얼마나 오래 걸릴지 말해줄래요?	
54	얼마나 오래 걸렸는지 까먹었어.	
55	얼마나 오래 걸리는지 모르겠어. 넌 얼마나 걸리는지 아니?	
56	우리가 여기에 얼마나 오래 있을 수 있는지 알아요?	
57	우리 서로 안지 얼마나 오래 됐는지 몰라. (그거) 매우 오래 됐어. 우리 어렸을 때부터, 친구였어.	
58	이게 뭐 하는건지 (원래!) 말해줄래요?	(물건이) 하다 = 기능
59	내 선글라스가 없어. 어디다 뒀는지 까먹었어.	없어 = 못 찾겠어
60	내가 뭐 말하려고 했었는지 까먹었었는데. 넌 내가 뭐 말하려고 했는지 어떻게 알았어?	

61	내가 예전엔 이걸 어떻게 했었는지 모르겠다.	
62	뭘 찾고 있는지 말해줄래요?	
63	내가 왜 그랬는지 모르겠어. 내가 왜 그 말 했는지 모르겠어.	
64	제가 얼마나 오래 기다려야 되는지 말해줘요.	
65	여기서 거기에 어떻게 갈 수 있는지 말해줄래요?	
66	이거 어디서 샀는지 기억이 안나.	
67	우리 서로 또 언제 볼 수 있는지 모르겠어.	
68	넌 무슨 생각하고 있는지 알고 싶어.	
69	이거에 대한 너의 생각이 뭔지 알고 싶어요.	
70	어떻게 그런 일이 생겼는지 모르겠어. 언제 그런 일이 생긴 건지 넌 아니?	

71	넌 뭐 주문하고 싶은지 말해줄래?	
72	우리가 얼마 내야 되는지 알려줄래요?	
73	내 기분이 어떤지 모르겠어.	기분이 들다 feel
74	내가 왜 오해를 했었는지 모르겠어.	오해하다 misunderstand
75	내가 뭐 사려고 했었는지 까먹었어. 집에다가 목록을 두고 왔어.	목록 a/the list
76	나 이거 가진지 얼마나 오래 됐는지 모르겠어.	
77	쟤네들은 어디 가는 건지 궁금하네.	
78	난 몇 시에 잤는지 모르겠어.	자다 go to sleep
79	내가 널 어떻게 도울 수 있는지 알고 싶어.	
80	이걸 어떻게 해결할지 모르겠어. 내가 이걸 해결할 수 있을지 궁금하다.	해결하다 fix/solve

"if/whether"

☞ 오른쪽 힌트를 이용해서, 직접 문장을 만들어보세요!

81	나 이거 해야 되는 건지 아닌지 모르겠어.	
82	너 이거 할 수 있는지 말해줘.	
83	너 그거 벌써 했는지 알고 싶어.	
84	**너 그거 해봤는지 말해줄래?**	
85	내가 그걸 하는 게 좋을지 모르겠어. 하는 게 더 나을까?	
86	**너 이거 하고 싶어 하는지 난 모르겠어.**	
87	제가 이거 해도 되는지 궁금해요.	
88	**우리 이거 할지 확실하지 않아요.**	
89	그 애 뭔가 하고 있는지 궁금하다. 그 애한테 해야 되는 말이 (뭔가) 있는데.	
90	**그 애 이거 좋아하는지 (아닌지/혹시) 아니?**	

"if/whether"

☞ 오른쪽 힌트를 이용해서, 직접 문장을 만들어보세요!

91	이거 되는지 모르겠어. 안 쓴지 좀 됐어. 해봐야 돼.	좀 for a while
92	내일 비가 올지 아니? 내일 세차 하려고 했었는데.	세차하다 wash the car
93	너도 올 건지 말해줘. 너 오면, 나도 올게.	
94	그 애 이거 먹어봤는지 모르겠네. 그래서 이거 좋아하는지 모르겠어.	먹어보다 try
95	나 괜찮아 보이는지 말해줄래? 나 어때 보여?	
96	내일 찾으러 가도 되는지 알고 싶어요.	
97	그 애 한국말 하는지 알아?	
98	나도 가야 되는 건지 모르겠어. 가고 싶지 않아. 하지만, 가야 된다면, 갈 거야.	
99	우리가 옳은 일을 한 건지 모르겠어.	옳은 일을 하다 do the right thing
100	제가 뭔가 잘못했는지 알고 싶어요.	뭔가 잘못 하다 do something wrong

Review

복습강의 MP3

Positive (긍정)	Negative (부정)	Question (의문)
Do/Go …. [동사 바로]	Don't	-
해, 하세요	하지 마, 하지 마세요	-
I used to	I didn't use to	Did you use to?
옛날엔 했었는데… (지금은 안 해)	옛날엔 안 했었는데… (지금은 해)	옛날엔 했었어?
I was going to	I wasn't going to	Were you going to?
하려고 했었는데… (안 했어)	안 하려고 했었는데… (했어)	하려고 했었어?
There is	There isn't	Is there?
있어	없어	있어?
There was	There wasn't	Was there?
있었어	없었어	있었어?
There will be	There won't be	Will there be?
있을 거야	없을 거야	있을까?

기초영어 1000문장 말하기 연습 3

01	엄마는 저녁 준비하느라 바빠.
02	우리 저녁 준비해야 돼.
03	그거 준비하는데 3시간 걸렸어.
04	오늘밤은 시험을 위해 준비하고 싶어.
05	우리 같이 인터뷰를 위해 준비하는 게 좋을 것 같아.
06	내가 뭔가 준비할 게.
07	지금 점심 준비할거야.
08	난 케익을 준비했어.
09	그 애가 우릴 위해 뭔가 준비할 지도 몰라.
10	짧은 연설을 준비하려고 했었는데… [짧은 연설 a speech]
11	내가 집에 왔을 때, 엄마는 저녁 준비하고 있었어.
12	시험을 위해 준비할 시간이 충분히 있어.
13	너가 이걸 어떻게 준비한 건지 알고 싶어.
14	우리 그 애를 위한 깜짝 파티를 준비했어. 그 애 놀랄 거야.
15	이 시험을 위해 어떻게 준비를 해야 하는지 모르겠어.

정답확인 : P 306

16	난 아무것도 준비 안 했는데.
17	그 애 시험을 위해 준비 안 했어.
18	그걸 위해 아무것도 준비하지 않아도 돼.
19	지금 면접을 위해 준비하는 거 아니야. 나 그건 아직 시작도 안 했어. [도, 조차도 even]
20	이거 준비하는 거 쉽지 않았어.
21	아무것도 준비하지 못 했어요.
22	우린 미래를 (위해) 대비하고 있지 않아요. 우린 이것에 대해 뭔가를 해야 합니다.
23	이거 준비하는데 오래 안 걸렸어.
24	너 (자꾸) 그러면, 나중엔 아무것도 준비할 시간이 없을 거야.
25	그 애 시험을 위해 준비하고 있는지 모르겠네.
26	넌 뭐 준비 할래?
27	모두가 뭔가를 준비하고 있는데. 우리는 뭘 준비할 거야?
28	내가 뭘 준비하는 게 좋을까?
29	우리 시험을 위해서 같이 준비해도 돼?
30	면접 위해 준비했니?

31	제가 뭘 준비해야 하는지 말해줄래요?
32	점심 준비하는 거야? 내 도움 필요해?
33	너라면, 이걸 위해 어떻게 준비할 거야? 너라면 어떻게 준비할지 알고 싶어.
34	이걸 위해 어떻게 준비하려고 했었어?
35	어떻게 혼자서 이걸 준비했어?
36	우리 뭐 준비해야 돼? 넌 우리가 뭘 준비해야 되는지 알아?
37	이걸 준비할 시간이 있었어? 이거 너무 고마워. 이거 준비하는데 얼마나 걸렸어?
38	최선을 희망하되, 최악에 대해 대비하세요.
39	우리 최악에 대비해야 돼.
40	전 최악의 상황에 대비하고 싶어요.
41	최악의 상황에 대비하는 것이 좋은 생각입니다.
42	우린 이미 최악의 상황에 대비했어.
43	모두가 최악에 대비하고 있어.

보안 검사 통과

Please take off your shoes and belt. And put them in the tray.

Remove any electrical goods/items from your bag.

Take out your wallet and keys.

Empty your pockets and put the contents in the tray.

Put the trays and your items/luggage on the conveyor belt.

Go/Pass/Walk/Step through the metal detector.

Stretch (out) your arms. / Put your arms out.

-

Can you have your ID ready?

If there is anything in your pocket, take them out and put them

in the tray.

Can I see your ID and your boarding pass?

Can you put all your belongings in the tray?

Are you wearing a belt?

Do you have a laptop?

Did you remove any electronic devices from your carry-on luggage?

Do you have anything in your pockets?

Do you have any liquids?

Is there anything sharp in your bags?

Do you have any electrical goods/items?

Do you have any sharp objects?

Can you put your wallet, laptop and all the metallic items in the tray?

Can you go through the metal detector?

Everything is fine. You are good to go.

보안 검사 통과

신발과 벨트를 벗어 주세요. 그리고 트레이에 넣으세요.

가방에서 전자 제품[electrical goods/items]을 빼세요.
[빼다, 제거하다 remove]

지갑과 키를 꺼내세요. [꺼내다 take out]

당신의 주머니를 비우고, 그 내용물을 트레이에 담으세요. [비우다 empty 내용물 the contents]

트레이와 당신의 짐을 컨베이어 벨트에 올려 주세요. [컨베이어 벨트 conveyor belt]

금속 탐지기[the metal detector]를 지나가세요. [지나가다 go through]

팔을 벌리세요. [벌리다 stretch/put-out]

-

신분증을 준비해 주시겠어요? [준비하다 have-ready]

주머니에 아무것이라도 있다면, 꺼내서 트레이에 넣으세요.

아이디와 탑승권을 볼 수 있을까요?

당신의 모든 소지품을 트레이에 넣어줄래요?

벨트를 착용하고 계신가요?

노트북을 가지고 있나요? [노트북 a laptop]

당신의 기내 수화물 가방에서 전자제품[electronic devices] 제거하

셨나요?

주머니에 아무것이라도 가진 게 있나요?

액체를 가지고 있나요?

가방안에 날카로운 것 [anything sharp]이 있나요?

전자제품을 가지고 있어요?

날카로운 물건들[sharp objects]을 가지고 있나요?

지갑, 노트북, 그리고 모든 금속제품[metallic items]을 트레이에

넣어 줄래요?

금속 탐지기를 지나가 줄래요?

모든 게 좋아요. 당신은 가셔도 좋아요.

보안 검사 통과

A: Are you wearing any jewelry?

B: No, I am not wearing anything.

A: Raise your arms please. I am going to scan your body.

B: I had a surgery a few years ago and I have a pin in my body.

A: That's fine. You are all set. You can go.

-

A: Is this your bag? I have to open it up and look inside (it).

Can you open your luggage?

B: What's this? You can't take any sharp objects on the plane.

A: I'm sorry. I forgot to take it out.

B: You are all set. You are good to go. (/Off you go.)

보안 검사 통과

A: 액세서리를 하고 계시나요?

B: 아니요. 아무것도 착용하고 있지 않아요.

A: 팔을 올려주세요. 당신의 몸을 스캔할 거 에요.

B: 몇 년 전에 수술을 했고, 제 몸 안에 핀이 있어요. [수술하다 have a surgery]

A: 괜찮아요. 당신은 다 되었어요. [다 된 all set] 가셔도 돼요.

-

A: 이게 당신 가방인가요? 열어보고 안을 봐야 합니다. 짐을 열어 주시겠어요?

B: 이게 뭐지요? 날카로운 물건들을 비행기로 가져갈 수 없습니다. [날카로운 물건 sharp objects]

A: 죄송합니다. 꺼낸 다는 것을 깜빡했습니다.

B: 당신은 다 되었습니다. 당신은 가셔도 좋아요.

Unit

7

의문의 문장을 또 다른 문장에 넣어 표현하고 싶을 때

'간접의문2- be동사'

이번 유닛에서는 be동사가 들어간 의문문이 다른 긍정이나 부정, 혹은 의문문에 들어간 문장들을 연습해 볼 거예요.

'Be'동사의 경우 의문문에서 다른 조동사를 사용하지 않고, 자리만 바꾸어서 사용했기에, 간접의문문에서는 다시 원래대로 자리를 바꾸어 주면 됩니다.

Indirect questions

I know	
I have to know	
I want to know	
I don't know	where the bus stop is.
I forgot	의문사 + 주어 + 동사
I don't/can't remember	
Tell me	
Do you know	
Can you tell me	

이렇게 만듭니다!

원래 말하고 싶은 문장 바로 뒤에 의문사 + 주어 + 동사를 넣어요.

> 몇 시인지 아니?
> **Do you know what time it is?**

<주의>

'의문사'가 없다면 **'if/whether'**(혹시/그런지 아닌지)를 넣어야 돼요!

> 그게 문제가 될지 모르겠어.
> **I don't know if/whether it will be a problem.**

<be동사 비교>

It is good.

It was good.

It has been good.

It is going to be good.

It will be good.

It has to be good.

It used to be good.

It was going to be good.

It may/might be good.

It would be good.

정답확인 : P 308

01	나 그거 뭔지 정확히 알아. 뭔지 알고 싶어?	정확히, 정확하게 exactly
02	그게 언제 였는지 생각이 안 나.	생각이 안 나 = 기억이 안 나/못 해
03	그게 얼마나 오래된건지 모르겠네. (그거) 몇일 되었어.	
04	이게 얼마일지 상상이 안 가. 비쌀 것 같아.	상상이 안 가 = 상상을 못하겠어
05	그게 예전엔 어디에 있었는지 까먹었어.	
06	저는 그게 언제일지 알고 싶어요.	
07	네가 왜 슬퍼했었는지 궁금해. 말해줄래? 너 많이 울었어.	
08	난 너가 몇살인지 알고 싶어. 추측하고 싶지 않아요. 몇살인지 말해줄 수 있어요?	추측하다 guess
09	우리가 지금 어디 있는 건지 모르겠어. 우리 길을 잃은지도 몰라.	길을 잃은 lost
10	몇 시였는지 기억이 안 나.	

11	무슨 색이었는지 말해줄래요?	
12	얼마나 먼지 알아야 돼. 가까운 데로 가고 싶어.	가까운 곳 somewhere close
13	저는 그게 언제 다 될지 알고 싶어요.	
14	너 어디 갔다 왔는지 말해줘. 어디 갔다 왔어?	
15	그게 얼마였는지 기억나? 거기에 돈 많이 썼니?	쓰다 spend money on
16	그 애 어떤지 궁금하다. 그 애 안 본 지 오래됐어.	
17	그게 어땠는지 알고 싶어. 좋은 시간 보냈니?	
18	너 어떻게 지냈는지 말해줄래? 바빴니?	
19	그게 어떨지 궁금해. 아주 멋질 거야.	
20	그게 예전엔 얼마였었나 잊었어. 가격이 예전엔 높았었지.	

21	너 어제 어디 있었는지 알아. 너 공원에 있었잖아. 나 너 거기에서 봤어.	
22	어느 길일지 확실하지 않아. 누군가한테 물어봐야겠다.	
23	난 그게 누군지 알아. 누군지 알고 싶어?	
24	너 여기 온지(=있은지) 얼마나 오래됐는지 말해줄래? (그거) 오래됐니?	
25	내가 예전엔 왜 이걸 무서워했었는지 이해가 안 가. 예전엔 많은 것들을 무서워했었어.	무서워하는 scared/afraid of
26	그게 얼마나 오래전이 있었는지 모르겠어. 아주 오래전이었어.	얼마나 오래전 how long ago
27	그 애 어느 나라 사람인지 모르겠어. (=어디 출신인지)	
28	그 애 사무실로 언제 돌아올지 말해줄래요?	돌아오는 back to
29	너 여기 몇번 와봤는지 궁금해.	
30	그게 예전엔 어땠는지 생각이 안 나.	

31	이게 무슨 사이즈인지 알고 싶어요. 라지예요? 작아 보이는데.	
32	얼마나 좋았는지 말해 봐.	얼마나 좋은 how good
33	예전엔 얼마나 컸었는지 모르겠어.	얼마나 큰 how big
34	그게 몇 시 일지 정확히 알아야 돼.	
35	쟤는 어디 갔다 왔는지 궁금하다.	
36	지금 몇 시인지 모르겠어. 난 지금 핸드폰이 없어. 차에 두고 왔어.	
37	이것들이 얼마였는지 아니?	
38	화장실이 어디에 있는지 말해줄래요?	
39	그게 얼마나 어려웠었는지 넌 몰라. 넌 안 해봤잖아.	얼마나 어려운 how hard
40	그게 얼마나 어려울지 상상이 안 가. 하지만, 넌 이거 이겨낼 수 있어.	이겨내다 overcome

41	너 왜 늦었는지 말해봐.	
42	넌 너가 10년 후에 어디에 있을지 알아?	10년후 in 10 years from now
43	이게 어디 있었는지 말해줄래? 어디서 찾았어?	
44	그 애 지금 어디 있는지 몰라. 넌 그 애 어디 있는지 알아? 어디 갔어?	
45	어느 거였는지 까먹었어.	
46	어느 거인지 기억이 안 나. 어느 게 내꺼니?	
47	나 이 사진에서 몇살이었는지 모르겠어. 20대 였어.	20대 in one's 20s
48	이게 누구 차인지 알아요?	누구(의) 차 whose car
49	이게 왜 여기 있는 건지 궁금하네. 네가 여기다 뒀어?	
50	그게 왜 였는지 알아? 그 이유를 알고 싶다.	

51	이게 왜 이런 건지 알고 싶어요. 나 아무것도 안 만졌는데…	이런 like this
52	너가 뭐에 대해 걱정했는지 알아. 하지만, 잘 됐잖아. 괜찮아. 그건 그만 걱정해.	잘 되다 work out (well)
53	거기 몇번 가봤는지 확실하지 않아. 많이 가봤어.	몇번 how many times
54	왜 내가 여기 있는지 모르겠어. 널 위해서 여기 왔지. 하지만, 여기 있기 싫어.	
55	이것들이 왜 다른지 모르겠어요. 차이점이 뭔지 설명해줄래요?	(그) 차이점 the difference
56	왜 화가 났었는지 이해해요. 사과하고 싶어요.	
57	내 선글라스가 어디에 있을까. (=어디 있는지 궁금하네.) 내가 어디다 놨지? 넌 어디에 있는지 알아?	
58	그게 얼마나 힘들지 이해가 가요. 이거 금방 끝날 거예요. 강해져요.	얼마나 힘든 how hard/ difficult 끝나는 over
59	너의 계획이 뭔지 말해줘. 대안 있어?	대안, 첫 계획이 실패할 경우 의 다른 계획 plan B
60	우린 그게 지금까지 어땠는지 알아야 합니다. 우린 그걸 바꿀 수 있어요. 우린 그걸 더 낫게 만들 수 있어요.	지금까지 so far

61	그 애 결혼했는지 알아?	결혼한 married
62	그게 거짓말이었는지 궁금해. 하지만, 거짓말 할 이유가 없잖아.	거짓말 a lie 거짓말 하다 lie
63	나 거기 가봤는지 확실하지 않아.	
64	그게 내일 열지 알고 싶어. 오늘 가야 되나?	
65	좋은 생각인지 아닌지 모르겠어.	좋은 생각 a good idea
66	그게 내 잘못이었는지 궁금해.	
67	여기서 수영을 해도 안전할지 말해줄래요?	
68	그거 재미있었는지 알고 싶어. 전부다 말해줘. 하나도 빼지말고.	빼다 leave out 하나도, 아무것도 anything
69	그게 더 나을 지 궁금하다. 어떡할까? (=뭘 하는게 좋을까?/뭘 할까?)	
70	이것들이 같은 건지 말해줄래? 나한텐 이것들 같아 보여.	

"if/whether"

☞ 오른쪽 힌트를 이용해서, 직접 문장을 만들어보세요!

71	그게 가능한 건지 알고 싶어요. 언제 가능한 건지 또한 말해줄래요?	또한 말해줄래요? Can you also tell me
72	그게 가능했는지 궁금해요.	
73	그렇게 하는 게 가능할지 아니?	
74	예전엔 그게 가능했는지 알고 싶어. 그게 어떻게 가능했지?	
75	너 괜찮은지 알고 싶어. 괜찮아? 얘기할 누군가가 필요하면, 아무때나 전화해.	
76	그 애 괜찮았는지 모르겠네. 걱정하는 것처럼 보였는데.	
77	그 애가 지금 바쁜지 모르겠어. 바쁠지도 몰라. 내가 그 애 볼 때, 그 애한테 말할게.	
78	이게 금방 끝날지 궁금해. 빨리 끝날수록, 좋은데.	끝나는 over 빨리 끝날수록 좋다. The sooner, the better.
79	이게 최선인지 모르겠어. 어떻게 생각해? 우리가 뭘 하는게 좋을 것 같아?	최선 the best
80	그게 최선이었는지 알고 싶어. 내가 할 수 있었던 게 (아무거나) 있었을까?	

81	여기 근처에 은행이 있는지 혹시 아세요?	
82	문제가 있었는지 난 알아야겠어. 문제 있었어?	
83	충분한 시간이 있을지 알고 싶어요.	
84	가능성이 있는 건지 말해줘요. 가능성이 있다면, 그거에 대해 뭔가 하고 싶어요.	
85	이유가 있었는지 모르겠어. 그 이유가 뭐였는데?	
86	차가 막히는지 모르겠네.	
87	방법이 있었는지 알아?	
88	사람이 많은지 말해줄래요? 사람 얼마나 있어?	
89	사람이 많았는지 말해줘. 몇 명 있었어?	
90	사람이 많을지 궁금하네. 사람 얼마나 올까? (=몇 명 있을까?) 많을 수록 좋은데.	

91	이 근처에 ATM 있는지 모르겠네. 못 봤는데. (=본적이 없어)	
92	학교에서 문제가 있었나 모르겠어. 그애 집에 왔을때, 뭔가 달라 보였어.	
93	이거에 대한 해결책이 있는지 알고 싶어요.	해결책 a solution to
94	사람 몇 명 있었는지 모르겠어. 세지 않았어.	세다 count
95	사람 몇 명 있을지 알아? 수천 명이 있을 거야.	수천 명 thousands of people
96	반에 학생이 몇 명 있는지 말해줄래요?	
97	거기 볼 게 많은지(=많은 것들이 있는지) 알아? 큰 도시야?	
98	이거 끝나면, 질문할 기회가 있을지 궁금하네.	끝나는 over
99	너가 하고 싶은 게 (아무거라도) 있는지 말해줄래?	
100	내가 할수 있는 게 (뭔가) 있는지 알고 싶어요. 돕고 싶어.	

Positive (긍정)	Negative (부정)	Question (의문)
Do/Go ···. [동사 바로]	Don't	-
해, 하세요	하지 마, 하지 마세요	-
I used to	I didn't use to	Did you use to?
옛날엔 했었는데… (지금은 안 해)	옛날엔 안 했었는데… (지금은 해)	옛날엔 했었어?
I was going to	I wasn't going to	Were you going to?
하려고 했었는데… (안 했어)	안 하려고 했었는데… (했어)	하려고 했었어?
There is	There isn't	Is there?
있어	없어	있어?
There was	There wasn't	Was there?
있었어	없었어	있었어?
There will be	There won't be	Will there be?
있을 거야	없을 거야	있을까?

01	지금 나갈게.
02	우리 지금 나가도 돼.
03	너 지금 나가야 돼. 안 그러면, 늦을 거야.
04	나도 지금 나가지 뭐.
05	너 오자 마자, 우리 나갈 수 있어.
06	나 지금 나가.
07	그 애 벌써 나갔어.
08	내가 들어올 때, 그 애는 나가고 있었어.
09	오늘밤에 친구들이랑 나갈지도 몰라.
10	예전엔 매 주말마다 나갔었는데.
11	그 앤 매일 밤 나가. 어디 가는지 궁금하다.
12	나갈 시간이야.
13	어젯밤 내 친구들이랑 나가려고 했었는데. 못 했어.
14	나도 너랑 나가고 싶었지. 근데, 어딘가 가야됐어. 미안.
15	난 오늘밤에 친구들이랑 나갈 거야. 우리 재미있게 놀 거야. [재미있게 놀다 have fun]

정답확인 : P 313

16	나가기 싫어.
17	난 지금 안나가.
18	그 앤 잘 안 나가.
19	너가 원하지 않으면, 우리 안 나가도 돼.
20	너 없이는 안 나갈 게. 널 기다릴게.
21	너 혼자 나가지 않는 게 좋을 것 같아.
22	그 애 아직 안 나갔어.
23	어제 안 나갔었어. 그럴 기분이 아니었어. [(할)기분이다 feel like]
24	어제 안 나가려고 했었는데. 그 애가 계속 전화했어.
25	밖에 안 나가 본지 오래 됐어.
26	그 애 나갔는지 모르겠어.
27	넌 예전에 매일 나가지 않았잖아.
28	오늘밤엔 우리 안 나갈 수도 있어.
29	오늘은 안 나갈 거야. 집에 있을 거야.
30	그 애 몇 시에 나갔는지 말해줄래요?

31	Tim 나갔어? 그 애 언제 나갔어?
32	나도 나가야 돼?
33	친구랑 나가도 돼요?
34	우리 지금 나갈까?
35	너 지금 나가는 거야? 어디가?
36	너라면, 그 애랑 나갈 거야? (데이트 의미)
37	언제 나갈 거야?
38	몇 시에 나가려고 했었어?
39	우리 이제 나가도 되는건지 말해줄래요?
40	날 위해서 위험을 감수하지 마.
41	내가 널 위해서 위험을 감수했어.
42	너 위험을 감수하고 있는 거야.
43	날 위해 위험을 감수하지 않아도 돼.

티켓 구매

A: We are going to go to the zoo tomorrow morning. I want to know if you have any information about/on the zoo.

B: Yes, we have a brochure. I will give one to you.

A: Thanks. Do I have to buy tickets in advance or can I walk up and buy them?

B: You can walk up and buy tickets. However, I think it will be better to buy tickets online. You don't have to wait at the ticket counter, and you can save some money as well. I can help you with that if you need some assistance.

A: Do you know how much the tickets are?

B: The admission/entrance fees are here on this page.

A: Thanks. This is very helpful. I also want to visit the S Gallery. Do you know if there is an entrance fee?

B: It's free of charge.

A: That's good.

B: Is there anything else I can help you with?

A: No, there isn't. Thank you very much.

A: I would like to get 3 tickets to Boston, please.

B: Sure. Would you like 3 adult tickets?

A: I'm travelling with my child. She is 7. Can I get/have two

adults and one child?

A: 저희 내일 아침에 동물원에 갈 거예요. 동물원에 관한 정보를 가지고 있는지 알고 싶어요.

B: 네, 저희 브로셔가 있어요. 하나 드릴게요.

A: 고마워요. 티켓을 미리 사야 하나요 아님 가서 사도 되나요?

[가서 사다 walk up and buy]

B: 가서 사도 돼요. 하지만, 인터넷으로 사는게 더 나을 것 같아요. 매표소[the ticket counter]에서 기다리지 않아도 되고요, 돈도 절약할 수 있어요. 도움[some assistance]이 필요하시면, 제가 그거 도와드릴 수 있어요.

A: 티켓들이 얼마인지 아세요?

B: 입장료가 이 페이지 여기에 있어요. [입장료 admission/entrance fees]

A: 고마워요. 이게 도움되네요. 전 S 갤러리 또한 방문하고 싶어요. 입장료가 있는지 아세요?

B: 무료예요. [무료, 공짜인 free of charge]

A: 좋네요.

B: 제가 도와드릴 수 있는 게 (아무거라도) 다른 게 있나요?

A: 없어요. 정말 고마워요.

A: 보스턴 (가는) 티켓 세 장을 사고 싶어요.

B: 네, 성인 티켓 세 장을 드릴까요? [드릴까요 Would you like~?]

A: 전 제 아이와 여행을 하는데요. 7살이에요. 성인 두 장 하고 아이 하나 주세요.

티켓 구매

_____

A: Could I get 3 tickets, please?

B: Will that be 3 adults?

A: I have a child.

B: Children under 14 years old can get child tickets. And

children under 4 don't need tickets.

A: My daughter is 11. So, 2 adults and one child, please.

B: Are you a member? Do you have a membership card?

A: No, I'm not a member. I don't have a membership card.

B: Alright. Your total is 54.

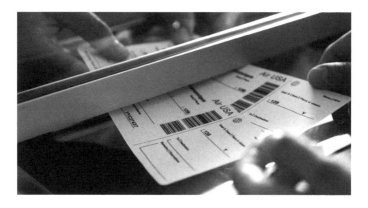

A: I'd like to buy a one way ticket to Boston, please.

B: When would you like to leave?

A: When is the next train?

B: There is a train at 8.

A: Ok, I will take that.

B: Would you like to travel 1st class or 2nd class?

A: Can you tell me how much they are?

B: The 1st class is 120, and the 2nd class is 80.

A: I will take the first class, please. How long does it take to get to Boston? Can you tell me what time I will arrive in Boston?

B: It takes 6 hours to get to Boston. So, you will arrive at 2.

티켓 구매

A: 티켓 세 장 주세요.

B: 성인 세 명일까요?

A: 아이가 있어요.

B: 14살 미만 아이들은 어린이 티켓을 살 수 있어요. 그리고 4살 미만 아이들은 티켓이 필요 없어요. [14세 미만 아이들 children under 14]

A: 제 딸은 11살이에요. 그러니, 성인 둘 과 아이 하나요.

B: 회원이세요? 회원카드가 있어요?

A: 아니요, 전 회원이 아니에요. 회원 카드 없어요.

B: 네. 총 54입니다. [총 your/the total]

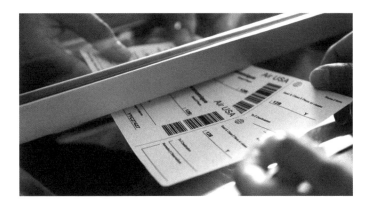

A: 보스턴(가는) 편도 티켓 하나 사고 싶어요.

B: 언제 출발하고 싶어요?

A: 다음 기차가 언제 에요?

B: 8시에 기차가 있어요.

A: 네, 그거로 할게요. [하다, 사다 take]

B: 1 등석 아니면 2 등석 여행 하실래요?

A: 그것들이 얼마인지 말해줄래요?

B: 1등석은 120이고요, 2등석은 80이에요.

A: 1등석으로 할게요. 보스턴 가는데 얼마나 걸리나요? 제가 몇

시에 보스턴에 도착할 지 말해 줄 수 있어요?

B: 보스턴 가는데 6시간 걸려요. 그래서, 2시에 도착할 거예요.

Unit

8

상대의 확인이나 동의를 구하는 질문을 하고 싶을 때

'하지, (그렇지)?'

무언가를 몰라서 질문하기 보다, 내가 알고 있는 것을 확인하거나 상대방의 동의를 구하기 위한 질문을 할 때, 작은 질문인 'question tag'을 문장 마지막에 붙일 수 있어요.

한국말 표현에서도 '이거 좋아하지?', '너무 비싸지 않니?'등의 형태의 문장들이 여기에 해당됩니다.

Positive (긍정)	Negative (부정)
긍정문, + 부정 tags	부정문, + 긍정 tags
You like it, don't you? You are going to come, aren't you?	You don't like it, do you? You aren't going to come, are you?

Intonation

모르거나 진짜 질문일 때 끝을 올림 ↗	You like it, don't you? ↗
확인하는 질문일 때 끝을 내림 ↘	You like it, don't you? ↘

ance noun. [18c:
intonation nour
voice in speech

메인 문장에서 사용한 조동사나 be동사에 tag를 붙이되,

긍정문에는 부정 tag를, 부정문에는 긍정 tag를 붙여요!

Positive (긍정)	Negative (부정)
저 가야 되지요, (그렇죠)?	전 안 가도 되지요, (그렇지요)?
I have to go, don't I?	I don't have to go, do I?
이거 예쁘지?	이거 안 예쁘지?
It is pretty, isn't it?	It isn't pretty, is it?

*조동사가 뭐예요??

- can, will, may, might, should 등

- 현재형에서 do/don't, 과거형에서 did/didn't, have.pp에서 have/haven't

*불규칙

1. I am, aren't I?

   I am the boss, aren't I?

2. Do/Don't (명령문), will you?

   Come quickly, will you?

3. Let's, shall we?

   Let's do this together, shall we?

긍정문, 부정 tag

☞ 오른쪽 힌트를 이용해서, 직접 문장을 만들어보세요!

훈련용 MP3

정답확인 : P 315

01	어렵지(, 그치)? 점점 어려워진다.	어려워지다 get hard
02	오늘 날씨 좋았다, 그렇지?	날씨 좋은 a beautiful/lovely day
03	돈 많이 들지, 그렇지 않니? 지금 그걸 할 여유가 있는지 모르겠어.	할/살 여유가 있다 afford
04	너 이거 좋아하지?	
05	내가 맞지(, 그렇지)? 그거 잘 안 됐잖아. 내가 맞고 싶진 않았는데… 내가 틀리고 싶었는데.	잘 되다 work out (well)
06	넌 중국에 가봤지? 어땠어? 올 여름에 우리 중국에 갈지도 몰라서.	
07	나 이거 해야 되지(, 그렇지)? 지금 할 수 있어.	
08	너 이거 찾고 있었지, 그렇지? 내가 청소할 때, 찾았어. 소파 밑에 있었어.	바닥 청소하다 vacuum the floor
09	사람 많았지(, 그치)?	
10	너도 올 거지, 그렇지? 너 안 오면, 나도 안 올 거야.	

긍정문, 부정 tag

☞ 오른쪽 힌트를 이용해서, 직접 문장을 만들어보세요!

11	사고였지(, 그렇지)? 일부러 그러지 않았잖아. 너 그럴 의도 아니었잖아, 그치?	일부러/고의로 on purpose 의도/의미이다 mean to
12	저거 위험해 보이지(, 그렇지)? 전혀 안전해 보이지 않아.	전혀 at all
13	너 그거 있지(, 그치)?	
14	나 이거 오늘 고치는 게 좋겠지?	
15	3일 걸렸었지(, 그러지 않았니)?	
16	너 요즘 바빴지, 그치?	
17	내가 아까 너한테 말했지(, 그치)?	아까 earlier
18	나 일찍이지(, 그치)? 시간 많다.	
19	나랑 같이 갈거지(, 그렇지)? 너 와야 돼. 혼자 가기 싫단말야.	
20	이거 살려고 했었지? 알고 있었어.	

21	너 깜빡했지(, 그렇지)? 그걸 어떻게 잊을 수 있어?	
22	너 차에 대해 많이 알지(, 그치)? 도움이 좀 필요한데.	
23	우리 여기서 기다리자, 그럴래?	
24	문 좀 열어, 어? 나 좀 들여 보내 줘.	들여 보내다 let-in
25	그 애 여기 있지(, 그치)? 어디 있어?	
26	넌 이미 알고 있었잖아(, 그치)? 넌 항상 그래. 넌 내게 아무것도 말하지 않아. 그게 문제야.	
27	너라면 가겠지, 그치? 난 이번에 왜 가기 싫은지 모르겠어. 가야겠지(, 그렇겠지)?	
28	차 많이 막혔지(, 그치)? 여기 오는데 얼마나 걸렸어?	
29	너 이거 봤지(, 그렇지?) 이거 말 안되지(, 그렇지 않니)? 정말 불공평해.	말이 되다 make sense 불공편한 unfair
30	나 예쁘지, 응?	

31	점심 먹었지(, 그치)? 점심으로 뭐 먹었어?	점심으로 for lunch
32	우리 서둘러야 되지?	
33	그거 증가하고 있지(, 그치)?	증가하다 increase
34	가자, 응?	
35	우리 지금 가는 게 좋겠다(, 그렇지)?	
36	너 그거 후회 되지(, 그치)? 하지만, 후회하지 않아도 돼. 넌 최선을 다했어. 모두 그걸 알아.	
37	이거 안 한 이유가 있지(, 그렇잖아)? 왜 안 했는지 말해줄래?	
38	내가 이겼지(, 그치)? 기분 너무 좋다.	기분 좋은 happy
39	일하고 있었지(, 그렇지)? 나 그냥 인사하러 왔어. 이따 봐.	인사하다 say hello
40	우리 또 곧 만날 거잖아요(, 그렇죠)? 잘 지내요.	잘 지내! Take care (of yourself).

긍정문, 부정 tag

☞ 오른쪽 힌트를 이용해서, 직접 문장을 만들어보세요!

41	우리 그거에 대해 뭔가 해야 되겠지(, 그렇지)? 점점 심각해 지는데.	
42	이거 갖고 싶었지(, 그치)?	
43	멀지(, 그렇지)? 내 차를 가져 가는 게 좋을 것 같아.	
44	우리 예전엔 거기 자주 갔었지(, 그렇지)? 우리 왜 거기 그만 가게 되었더라? 기억나니?	그만 하다 stop -ing
45	너라면 그냥 기다리겠지(, 그렇지)? 기다리기 정말 힘들어.	
46	그만해, 어?	
47	그 애가 이거 좋아할 것 같지(, 그렇지 않니)?	
48	나 늦었지(, 그렇지)? 미안해. 이런 일 다신 없을 거예요.	
49	내가 여기 있잖아, 어? 넌 혼자가 아니야.	
50	다음주에 만나자, 응? 다음주에 전화할게.	전화하다 give 사람 a call

부정문, 긍정 tag

☞ 오른쪽 힌트를 이용해서, 직접 문장을 만들어보세요!

51	저 이거 지금 안해도 되는거죠(, 그렇지요)? 지금은 시간이 없어요. 제가 할 수 있을 때, 할게요. 🔊	
52	**사실이 아니지(, 그치)? 믿기 어렵다.** 🔊	
53	너 어제 그거 못끝냈지, (그치)? 이해해. 너 어제 할거 많았잖아. 🔊	할 게 많다 = 할게 많은 것들이 있다
54	**아무말도 하지마, 알았지? 나한테 약속해야돼.** 🔊	
55	너 아직 그 애 안 만나봤지(, 그렇지)? 🔊	
56	**넌 아무한테도 말 안했지(, 그치)? 그앤 어떻게 알았지?** 🔊	
57	이거 지금 쓰는거 아니지요(, 그렇죠)? 🔊	
58	**그거 상관없지(, 그치)?** 🔊	상관있다 matter
59	아무것도 없었지(, 그치)? 🔊	
60	**너 여기 온지 오래되지 않았지(, 그치)?** 🔊	

부정문, 긍정 tag
☞ 오른쪽 힌트를 이용해서, 직접 문장을 만들어보세요!

61	너 몸이 안 좋지(, 그치)? 몸 안좋아 보여.	몸(컨디션)이 좋은, 잘있는 well
62	넌 아직 모르는 구나(, 그렇지)?	
63	시간 모자랐지(, 그치)?	
64	아무한테도 말 안할거지(, 그렇지)?	
65	그게 문제 아니었지(, 그치)? 뭐가 문제 였는지 궁금하다.	
66	문제 없었지(, 그렇지)?	
67	그거 크지 않아도 되는거지(, 그렇지)? 이게 맞을까?	(사이즈가) 맞다 fit
68	넌 오기 싫었지(, 그렇지)? 와줘서 고마워.	고마워 Thank you for
69	넌 안 오려고 했었지(, 그치)? 널 봐서 너무 좋았어.	
70	이거 오래 안 걸리겠지(, 그렇지)?	

71	이거 너꺼 아니지(, 그렇지)? 이게 누구의 책인지 궁금하다.	누구의 책 whose book
72	넌 그거 어디있는지 모르지(, 그치)? 그게 어디 간건지 궁금하네.	
73	우리 그 애한테 말 안 하는게 좋겠지(, 그치)? 그 애 기분 나빠할 걸.	기분 나빠하다 feel bad
74	늦지마, 알았지?	
75	이런 일 다신 없을 거지(, 그치)?	
76	넌 그거 별로였지(, 그치)?	별로다 = 좋아하지 않다
77	그 애 골프 안 치지(, 그렇지)?	
78	우리 이거 하면 안 되는 거지(, 그렇지)?	
79	나 지금 도움이 안 되는 거지(, 그치)? 내가 자리 비켜줄게.	자리 비키다, 방해 안하다 get out of one's way
80	넌 그 애랑 안 어울릴 거지(, 그렇지)? 나한테 약속해 줄 수 있어?	어울리다 hang out with

81	그거 나아지고 있지 않지(, 그렇지)? 그럴줄 알았어.	그럴줄 알았어. I thought so.
82	날 도와줄 시간 없지(, 그치)?	
83	오래 안 걸리지(, 그렇지)? 나 10분 밖에 없는데.	밖에 (없는), 딱 only
84	너 그거 안 잊어버렸지(, 그치)?	
85	아직 배 안 고프지(, 그치)?	
86	이거 안 될 것 같지(, 그치)? 이거 안 되면, 난 뭘 해야될까?	
87	가지마, 응? 나랑 같이 있어줄래?	
88	많이 나쁘진 않지(, 그렇지)?	많이/아주 나쁜 too bad
89	사람 많이 없지(, 그치)?	
90	그 애 만나기 싫지(, 그렇지)? 나도 그 애 만나기 싫어.	

부정문, 긍정 tag

☞ 오른쪽 힌트를 이용해서, 직접 문장을 만들어보세요!

91	이거 안 되지(, 그치)?	
92	내 이야기 하고 있던거 아니지, (그렇지)?	
93	기억 안 나지(, 그렇지)?	
94	너 나한테 말 안 할려고 했었지(, 그치)?	
95	그렇게 생각하지 마, 응?	그렇게 like that
96	거기 아직 안 가봤지(, 그치)? 나라면 이번엔 거기로 가겠어.	
97	내가 할 수 있는 게 (아무것도) 없지(, 그렇지)?	
98	돈 별로 안 들었지(, 그치)?	
99	지금 취소 안 되죠(, 그렇지요)?	안 되다 = 못 하다
100	너 나한테 화났던 거 아니지(, 그렇지)?	

Positive (긍정)	Negative (부정)	Question (의문)
Do/Go …. [동사 바로]	Don't	-
해, 하세요	하지 마, 하지 마세요	-
I used to	I didn't use to	Did you use to?
옛날엔 했었는데… (지금은 안 해)	옛날엔 안 했었는데… (지금은 해)	옛날엔 했었어?
I was going to	I wasn't going to	Were you going to?
하려고 했었는데… (안 했어)	안 하려고 했었는데… (했어)	하려고 했었어?
There is	There isn't	Is there?
있어	없어	있어?
There was	There wasn't	Was there?
있었어	없었어	있었어?
There will be	There won't be	Will there be?
있을 거야	없을 거야	있을까?

01	오늘 나랑 저녁 먹어, 응?
02	너랑 내일 저녁 하고 싶어. 내일 괜찮아?
03	우리 언제 저녁 해야지. [언제 someday]
04	다음주에 너랑 저녁 먹을 수 있어. 다음주에 보자.
05	나 친구랑 저녁 먹을 거야. 나 기다리지 마.
06	우리 지금 저녁 먹는게 좋겠어.
07	나 저녁 벌써 먹었어.
08	우리 저녁 먹고 있는데. 같이 먹을래?
09	난 보통 저녁 7시에 먹어.
10	내가 도착했을 때, 그 애들 저녁 먹고 있었어.
11	우리 여기서 저녁 먹지 뭐.
12	그 앤 예전에 저녁 먹으러 집에 왔었는데.
13	그 쇼 후에 우리 저녁 같이 먹을 수도 있어.
14	우리 저녁 같이 먹으려고 했었는데, 그 애 회사로 돌아가야 됐어.
15	우리 저녁 같이 먹자, 그럴래?

정답확인 : P 320

16	나 그 애랑 저녁 먹기 싫어.
17	우리 지금 저녁 안 먹는게 좋을 것 같아. 좀 일러.
18	우리 같이 저녁 안 먹을 거야. 내가 취소했어.
19	나 아직 저녁 안 먹었어.
20	그 애랑 저녁 같이 못 먹었어.
21	오늘은 저녁 안 먹으려고 했었는데… 모든 게 맛있었어.
22	너 저녁 안 먹었지 (, 그치)? 지금 뭔가 먹을래?
23	너 올때까지, 저녁 안 먹을 게.
24	그 앤 저녁 혼자 안 먹어.
25	지금 저녁 먹는 거 아니야. 너무 일러.
26	난 저녁 먹을 시간이 없었어. 하루 종일 바빴어.
27	우리 아직 함께 저녁 안 먹어봤어.
28	그 애 저녁 먹었는지 모르겠네.
29	우리 지금 저녁 먹어야 돼?
30	우리 어디서 저녁 먹을까?

31	저녁으로 뭐 먹고 싶은지 말해줄래? [저녁으로 for dinner]
32	우리 언제 같이 저녁 먹을 거야? 지금 말해줘.
33	나랑 저녁 먹을래?
34	저녁 먹었어?
35	지금 저녁 먹어?
36	넌 저녁 보통 몇 시에 먹어?
37	그 애랑 저녁 먹어서 좋았어?
38	저녁 먹고 있었어?
39	우리 어디서 저녁 먹는게 좋을 것 같아?
40	언제 나랑 저녁 먹을 수 있는지 말해줄래?
41	너랑 같이 또 저녁 먹을 기회가 있을까?
42	예전엔 어디서 저녁 먹었었어?
43	너라면, 어디서 저녁 먹을 거야?

A: Where are you?

B: I'm almost there. I'll be there in 5 minutes.

A: Ok. See you soon.

B: I'm so sorry I'm late. Have you been waiting long?

A: I got here at 5 ish. I have been waiting for half an hour. Was there a traffic jam?

B: Yes, there was a lot of traffic. It took an hour to get here.

–

A: Hey, how's it going?

B: I'm great. How are you doing?

A: I'm good, thanks. I've been meaning to call you. It's so great to see you.

B: It is great to see you, too. I was going to call you last week.

–

A: What happened to your leg? Did you hurt yourself?

B: I hurt my ankle.

A: How did it happen?

B: I fell and sprained my ankle.

A: When did that happen?

B: It happened the day before yesterday.

–

A: What have you been doing all day?

B: I have been working all day.

A: But it's Saturday. Do you work on Saturdays?

B: No, I don't work on Saturdays. There was a project we had to finish. So, we all had to work today.

A: This is for you.

B: I have been looking for it. You are a lifesaver. Thank you.

일상

A: 어디야?

B: 나 거의 다 왔어. [= 넌 거의 거기야] 5분이면 도착해. [= 5분이면 거기 있을 거야]

A: 알았어. 금방 봐.

B: 늦어서 정말 미안해. 오래 기다렸어?

A: 5시쯤 왔어. [5시쯤 5 ish] 30분 기다렸어. 차 막혔니?

B: 어, 차가 많이 막혔어. 여기 오는데 1시간 걸렸어.

-

A: 안녕, 기분 어때?

B: 좋아. 넌 기분 어때?

A: 좋아, 고마워. 너한테 전화한 다는게… 너 보니 너무 좋다.

B: 너 봐서 좋아. 저번주에 전화하려고 했었는데.

-

A: 다리 왜 그래? [왜 그래? What happened to?] 다쳤니?

B: 발목을 다쳤어.

A: 어떻게 하다 그랬어? (=어떻게 그런 일이 생긴 거야?)

B: 넘어져서, 발목을 삐었어. [삐다 sprain]

A: 언제 그랬어? (= 언제 그런 일이 생긴 거야?)

B: 그제 그랬어. [그저께 the day before yesterday]

-

A: 오늘 하루 종일 뭐했어?

B: 하루 종일 일했어.

A: 하지만 토요일이잖아. 토요일에 일해?

B: 아니, 토요일에 일 안 해. 우리가 마무리해야 되는 프로젝트가

있었어. 그래서 우리 모두 오늘 일해야 됐어.

A: 이거 널 위한 거야.

B: 어, 나 이거 찾고 있었는데. 넌 생명의 은인이야. [생명의 은인 a

lifesaver] 고마워.

Unit

9

'지금까지' 하고 있는 걸 말하고 싶을 때

'하고 있었어(지금)' have/has been -ing

과거의 어느 시점부터 지금까지 연결이 되고(현재완료), 그 진행되는 행위에 초점이 맞추어 진 문장들은 현재완료(have p.p)의 진행(-ing) 형태인 'have been -ing'를 사용해요.

Positive (긍정)	Negative (부정)	Question (의문)
I We You They have been -ing	I We You They haven't been -ing	Have I we you they have been -ing
He She It has been -ing	He She It hasn't been -ing	Has he she it been -ing?
하고 있었어(지금).	안 하고 있었어.	하고 있었어?

함께 쓰이는 단어
for, since, how long

'have/has been'에 동사 + -ing를 넣어요.

Positive (긍정)	Negative (부정)	Question (의문)
기다리고 있었어. I have been waiting.	오래 기다리지 않았어. I haven't been waiting long.	얼마나 오래 기다렸어? How long have you been waiting?

am,is,are -ing vs have been -ing

I am reading a book.	'지금' 읽어.
I have been reading a book.	'지금' 읽고 있었어. (쭉~)

have p.p. vs have been -ing

I have read this book.	읽었어 / 읽어봤어. (결과, 끝)
I have been reading this book.	읽고 있었어. (읽는 행위 초점)

was/were -ing vs have been -ing

I was reading a book (when you came).	'그때' 읽고 있었어.
I have been reading a book.	'지금' 읽고 있었어.

Speaking Practice
1min

긍정문 I have been -ing
☞ 오른쪽 힌트를 이용해서, 직접 문장을 만들어보세요!

훈련용 MP3

정답확인 : P 322

01	자고 있었어. 어젯밤에 늦게 잤어. 언제 왔어?	
02	나 영어 배운지 2년 됐어. 영어 공부하는 거 재미있어.	
03	우리 2005년부터 이 집에서 살았어. 예전엔 마포에 살았었어, 여기 이사오기 전에.	
04	나 여기서 일한지 4년 됐어. 벌써 4년 됐다. 시간이 빨리 가.	(시간이) 빨리 가다 fly
05	그 애 졸업한 후로 거기서 일했어.	
06	나 2시부터 기다리고 있었어. 넌 어디 있었어?	
07	Pam은 아침 내내 자네.	아침내내 all morning
08	어디 갔다 왔어요? Pam이 계속 너 찾았어.	
09	나 이거 찾던건데. 고마워. 어디서 찾았어?	
10	하루종일 집 청소하고 있었어.	

긍정문 I have been -ing

☞ 오른쪽 힌트를 이용해서, 직접 문장을 만들어보세요!

11	피곤해. 차에 3시간이나 앉아있었어.	
12	다리 아프다. 오늘 하루 종일 걸었어.	
13	우리 오늘 공부 열심히 했어. (그거에 대해) 기분이 좋아.	
14	그 애 요즘 일 많이 했지. 너무 바빴어.	
15	Jim은 1시부터 지금까지 TV 보는 거야.	
16	나 요즘 네 생각 많이 했어.	
17	우리 정말 열심히 했는데… 왜 그들은 우리를 뽑지(=선택하지) 않았는지 모르겠어. 다음번엔 우리가 이길 거야.	열심히 하다 try hard
18	Tim은 영어 가르친지 6년 됐어. 훌륭한 선생님이야.	
19	나 그거 사용한지 오래 됐지. 난 다른 건 못 쓰겠어.	다른 거 anything else
20	나 거기 다닌지 몇 달 됐어.	

긍정문 I have been -ing

☞ 오른쪽 힌트를 이용해서, 직접 문장을 만들어보세요!

21	저 사람 정말 오래 이야기 하네. 지루하다.	정말 오래 for hours
22	나 집안 일 하고 있었어.	집안 일 하다 do the housework
23	나 요새 운동 좀 했지.	
24	나 하루 종일 너한테 전화했었는데…	
25	우리 네 얘기 하고 있었어.	
26	나 그거 생각하고 있었어. 근데 뭘 해야 할지 모르겠어.	
27	우리 지금은 뭔가 하고 있었어. 괜찮다면, 금방 다시 전화할게요.	
28	나 지금 2시간 째 요리하고 있어.	
29	그 애가 계속 나 도와주고 있어. 그 애 너무 괜찮지(,그렇지 않니)?	
30	피곤하다. 운전을 3시간이나 했어. 너도 피곤하지(,그치)?	

긍정문 I have been -ing

☞ 오른쪽 힌트를 이용해서, 직접 문장을 만들어보세요!

31	우리 영어 공부하고 있었어.	
32	나 이 차 운전한지 오래 됐어. 새 차 사고 싶어.	
33	우리 이 노래만 계속 들었잖아. 질린다. 다른 거 듣고 싶어.	질리는 tired/sick of 다른 거 something else
34	그 애 일자리 구하고 있었어. 요즘에 일자리 구하기 쉽지 않아.	일자리 구하다 look for a job 요즘 these days
35	그 애 25살 때부터 담배 폈어. 끊기 힘들 거야.	
36	나 어렸을 때부터 이거 해왔어. 쉬워.	
37	나 너에 대해 궁금해 하고 있었는데. 널 봐서 너무 좋다. 어떻게 지냈어?	궁금해 하다 wonder
38	내 흰 가방 봤어? 하루 종일 찾고 있는데. 어디에도 없어. (=어디에서도 찾을 수가 없어)	
39	우리 오늘 쉬지 않고 일했어. 쉬어도 되는지 알고 싶어.	쉬지않고 nonstop 쉬다 take a break
40	요즘엔 버스 타고 있어. 한 달전에 차 팔았어.	

41	오랜만이야. 전화를 한다는 게…(그럴 의도였는데)	한다는 게 = 할 의미/의도이다 mean to
42	미안. 저거 바꾼다는 게… 지금 할게.	
43	내가 그걸 한다는 게… 그걸 할 기회가 없었네.	
44	내가 저번주에 너한테 연락 하려고 했었는데, 미안해. 나 요즘 힘들어서…	힘들다, 힘든 시간을 보내 다 have a hard time
45	넌 정말 잘 해왔어. 난 너가 정말 자랑스러워.	
46	로맨틱 코메디 너무 많이 봤구나. 현실엔 그런 일 안 생겨.	로맨틱 코메디romantic comedies (rom coms) 현 실엔 in real life
47	누군지는 모르겠지만, 누군가가 계속 내 종이를 가져가 고 있어. 너 누군지 모르지, (그치)?	
48	비가 하루 종일 오네. 빗방울 소리가 난 좋아.	빗방울 소리 the sound of raindrops
49	밤새도록 눈이 내렸어. 밖에 모든 게 다 하얘.	
50	여기 화요일부터 눈이 내려.	

부정문 I haven't been -ing

☞ 오른쪽 힌트를 이용해서, 직접 문장을 만들어보세요!

51	아무것도 안 하고 있었어.	
52	그렇게 오래 기다리지 않았어요. 10분쯤 전에 도착했어요.	
53	우리 네 얘기 하고 있던 거 아니야.	
54	저 여기서 산지 그렇게 오래 되지 않았어요. 저번달에 여기로 이사했어.	
55	그 애 거기서 일한지 오래 되지 않았어.	
56	공부하고 있던 거 아니야. 책 읽고 있었어.	
57	그 애 영어 공부한지 오래 되지 않았어.	
58	우리 서로 이야기 안 한지 몇 일 됐어. 그 애 화나면, 말 안 해.정말 짜증나.	말하다, 얘기하다, 대화하다 talk/speak 짜증나는 annoying
59	나 그 애 생각 안 한지 좀 됐네.	좀 for a while
60	별거 안 하고 있었어.	별거 much

61	거기 안 다닌지 몇 일 됐어.	
62	안 자고 있었어. 명상하고 있었어.	명상하다 meditate
63	요즘에 기분이 좀 안 좋았어. 계속 기분이 다운 되어 있네.	
64	요즘 잠을 계속 잘 못 잤어. 피곤하다.	
65	우리 데이트한지 오래 되지 않았어. 우리 저번달에 처음 만났어. (그거) 한 달 됐네.	데이트하다 date
66	저 여기서 머문지 그렇게 오래 되진 않았어요. 3일 됐어 요. 한국에 다음주에 돌아 갈 거예요.	
67	우리 이 노래 안 들은지 오래됐다. 이게 예전에 우리가 가장 좋아하는 노래였는데…	
68	나 술 안 마신지 몇 일 되었어. 술 끊기로 했어.	술마시다 drink
69	나 이거 사용 안 한지 좀 됐어. 이거 되는지 모르겠다.	좀 for a while
70	운동 안 한지 몇 달 되었어. 다음달 부터 헬스장에 갈 거야.	

의문문 Have you been -ing?

☞ 오른쪽 힌트를 이용해서, 직접 문장을 만들어보세요!

71	뭐 하고 있었어?	
72	여기서 일한지 얼마나 오래 됐어?	
73	영어 공부한지 얼마나 오래 됐어? 영어 잘한다.	
74	무슨 생각하고 있었어? 내 생각 하고 있었어?	
75	여기서 산지 얼마나 오래 되었어? 언제 여기로 이사왔어?	
76	늦어서 미안해요. 오래 기다렸어요?	
77	얼마나 오래 기다렸어? 언제 왔어요?	
78	하루 종일 뭐했어요?	
79	이거 쓴지 얼마나 오래 됐어?	
80	거기 다닌지 오래 됐어? 얼마나 오래 됐어?	

의문문 Have you been -ing?

☞ 오른쪽 힌트를 이용해서, 직접 문장을 만들어보세요!

81	내 얘기 하고 있었어? 무슨 얘기 하고 있었는지 알고싶어.	
82	영화 보고 있었니? 좋은 영화야?	
83	이 차 낡아 보여. 이차 운전한지 오래됐어?	
84	자고 있었어? 졸린 목소리 인데.	목소리이다 sound
85	그애랑 같이 일한지 얼마나 됐어? 너 그애 잘 알아?	
86	뭐 만들고 있었어?	
87	이거 한지 얼마나 오래 됐어? 너 이거 잘한다!	
88	Tim은 영어 가르친지 얼마나 됐어? 그 애 경험 많아?	경험 많다 have a lot of experience
89	뭔가 하고 있었니? 내가 방해했어? 너가 원하면, 나중에 다시 올 수 있어.	
90	제가 잘 해오고 있는건가요?	

의문문 Have you been -ing?

☞ 오른쪽 힌트를 이용해서, 직접 문장을 만들어보세요!

91	너 눈 빨개. 울었어? 무슨 일이야?	무슨 일이야? What's up?
92	술 마셨어? 괜찮아?	
93	너 숨차하네. 뛰었어?	숨차는 out of breath
94	너 땀 흘리네. 운동했어?	땀흘리다 sweat
95	나 기다린거야? 나한테 할말 (뭔가) 있니?	
96	노래 불렀니?	
97	내가 널 마지막으로 본 게 (=본 이후로) 오래됐다. 뭐하고 지냈어?	
98	내 핸드폰 썼니? 내 핸드폰 어떻게 잠금 해제 했어?	잠금해제 하다 unlock
99	내 이메일 읽었어? 사생활 침해야.	사생활 침해 an invasion of privacy
100	비 왔나?	

Review

Positive (긍정)	Negative (부정)	Question (의문)
Do/Go …. [동사 바로]	Don't	-
해, 하세요	하지 마, 하지 마세요	-
I used to	I didn't use to	Did you use to?
옛날엔 했었는데… (지금은 안 해)	옛날엔 안 했었는데… (지금은 해)	옛날엔 했었어?
I was going to	I wasn't going to	Were you going to?
하려고 했었는데… (안 했어)	안 하려고 했었는데… (했어)	하려고 했었어?
There is	There isn't	Is there?
있어	없어	있어?
There was	There wasn't	Was there?
있었어	없었어	있었어?
There will be	There won't be	Will there be?
있을 거야	없을 거야	있을까?
I have been -ing	I haven't been -ing	Have you been -ing?
하고 있었어 (지금)	안 하고 있었어	하고 있었어?

01	내일 일할 수 있어요.
02	이번 주말에 난 일할 거야. 내가 끝내야 하는 프로젝트가 있어.
03	내일 나 일해야 되지 (, 그치)?
04	우리 지금 함께 일하고 있어. 우리 프로젝트 같이 하거든.
05	우리 내일 같이 일 할지도 몰라.
06	나도 예전엔 여기서 일했었어.
07	어제 일했어.
08	우리 같이 일하지 뭐.
09	그 앤 일 열심히 해. 일주일에 7일 일해. [일주일에 7일 7 days a week]
10	저번 주말에 나도 일하려고 했었는데, 내가 참석해야 되는 세미나가 있었어.
11	내가 왔을 때, 모두 벌써 일하고 있던데.
12	우리 같이 일하는 게 좋을 것 같아. 그래서 우리 일찍 끝낼 수 있게.
13	나 여기서 일 한지 2 년 됐어.
14	지금 일하고 있었지요 (, 그렇죠)? 전 신경 쓰지 마세요. [신경 쓰다 mind]
15	그 애 이번 주말에 일할지 모르겠어.

정답확인 : P 327

16	난 그 애랑 일하고 싶지 않아.
17	나 내일 일 안 할 거야. 난 내일 자유야. 너 하고 싶은 거 (뭔가) 있어?
18	난 더 이상 여기서 일 못 하겠어.
19	그 애 예전엔 일 열심히 안 했었는데. 많이 변했어.
20	우리 같이 일 안 할 수도 있어.
21	오늘밤은 우리 일 안 하는 게 좋을 것 같아. 모두들 피곤하고. 내일 시작하자, 응?
22	저번 주말에 나 일 안 했어.
23	어제 일 못 했어. 몸이 안 좋았어.
24	여기서 일한지 오래되지 않았어. 2달 전에 시작했어.
25	어제 몇 시간을 일한 건지 모르겠어.
26	지금 일하는 거 아니지 (, 그렇지)? 내가 너한테 말해줘야 되는게 뭔가 있어.
27	넌 어디서 일해?
28	내일 일해야 돼?
29	언제 일할 수 있는지 말해 줄래요?
30	어제 일했어? 몇 시간 일했어?

31	여기서 일 한지 얼마나 오래 됐어? 오래 됐어요?
32	여기 오기 전에 예전엔 어디서 일했었어?
33	내일은 어디에서 일할 거야?
34	여기서 왜 일하고 싶은 가요? 왜 이게 당신의 꿈의 직업인가요? [꿈의 직업 dream job]
35	지금 일해? 어디서 일하고 있어?
36	너랑 같이 일해도 돼? 난 항상 너랑 같이 일하고 싶었어.
37	너희 둘이서 알아서 해. [너희 둘 between you two]
38	우리 처음에는 의견이 일치하지 않았는데, 우리 함께 해결했어.
39	우리 처음에 만났을 땐, 많이 싸웠었어. 하지만, 우린 해결했어. 지금은 우리의 관계 좋아. [관계 relationship]
40	우리 함께 이거 해결할 수 있어요.
41	나 그거 해결했어.
42	우리 그거 지금 함께 해결하는 중입니다.

기내에서

A: Could you show me your boarding pass?

B: Yes, can you tell me where my seat is?

A: Your seat is right over there.

−

A: Excuse me, could I go through? My seat is over there.

B: Sure. I am sorry about that.

−

A: Could you help me put this bag in the overhead compartment/bin?

A: There is no room in the overhead bin. Could you tell me where I can store my bag?

−

A: Is it possible to change/switch seats with someone? My friend and I didn't get seats together. We would like to sit together.

B: I will check. It might be possible, but you have to wait until the plane takes off.

A: Could I get/have a pair of headphones?

Please put away your laptop.

Fasten your seatbelt.

Remove your headphones.

Turn off your phones and mobile devices.

Switch off all electronic devices.

Please return your seat to the upright position. We are about to

take off.

Could you please sit down? We are about to land.

기내에서

A: 탑승권 보여 주시겠어요?

B: 네, 제 자리가 어디인지 말해주실래요?

A: 당신의 좌석은 바로 저기에 있습니다.

-

A: 실례지만, 지나가도 될까요? 제 자리가 저기 거든요.

B: 물론이죠. 죄송합니다.

-

A: 이 가방을 머리 위 짐 칸 [overhead compartment/bin] 에 넣는 거
   도와 주실 수 있으세요?

A: 짐 칸에 자리가 없어 [too room] 요. 어디에 제 가방을 보관할 수
   있는지 말해 주실래요? [보관하다 store]

-

A: 누군가와 자리를 바꾸는 게 가능한가요? 제 친구랑 제가 좌석
   을 같이 얻지 않았어요. 저희 같이 앉고 싶어요.

B: 확인해 볼게요. 가능할 수도 있지만, 비행기가 이륙할 때까지
   기다리셔야 합니다. [이륙하다 take off]

A: 헤드폰 주세요. [헤드폰 a pair of headphones]

노트북을 넣어주세요. [넣다, 치우다 put away]

당신의 안전벨트를 매세요. [매다 fasten]

헤드폰을 빼세요. [빼다, 제거하다 remove]

당신의 전화기와 모바일 제품들을 꺼주세요.

모든 전자제품을 꺼주세요.

당신의 좌석을 똑바로 되돌려 [return to]주세요. [똑바로 the upright

position] 저희는 이륙하려고 합니다. [~하려고 하는 about to]

앉아 주시겠어요? 저희는 착륙하려고 합니다. [착륙하다 land]

기내에서

A: My headphones are not working. Could I have another pair?

A: I have a problem with my seatbelt. Can you help me with that?

A: I can't put my seat (back) up/upright. My seat is stuck.

A: It's chilly in here. I'm a bit cold. Could I get another blanket?

–

A: Can I get you something to drink?

B: What kind of drinks do you have?

A: We have coffee, tea, juice, coke and beer.

B: I'll have a beer, please.

A: Alright. Anything else?

B: No, that will be all. Thank you.

A: I will be right back with your beer.

기내에서

A: 제 헤드폰이 안 됩니다. 다른 헤드폰 주세요.

A: 제 안전벨트에 문제가 있어요. 그거 좀 도와줄 수 있어요?

A: 제 의자를 못 올리겠어요. [올리다 put-up] 제 의자가 움직이지

않아요. [움직이지 않는, 낀 stuck]

A: 여기 안이 쌀쌀합니다. 제가 조금 추워요. 제가 담요 하나 더

가질 수 있을까요?

-

A: 뭔가 마실 것 드릴까요? [드릴까요? Can I get you]

B: 어떤 종류의 음료가 있어요?

A: 커피, 차, 주스, 콜라랑 맥주 있습니다.

B: 맥주로 할게요.

A: 네. 다른 것은요? [Anything else]

B: 없어요, 그게 다 일 겁니다. 고맙습니다.

A: 당신의 맥주를 가지고 바로 돌아올 게요. [~를 가지고, ~와 with]

Unit

Unit 10

상대의 의향을 물어보면서 허락을 구하거나
부탁하고 싶을 때

Do you mind?

허락이나 부탁하는 표현으로 일상생활에서 자주 사용 되는 'Do/Would you mind?'를 이번 단원에서 연습 해볼게요.

'Mind'가 들어간 이 표현은 직역하면 '~하면 신경이 쓰이겠니/마음에 안들겠니?'로, 직접적으로 허락이나 부탁하는 'can/may/would'등과 다르게, 상대가 'No'라고 대답할 때 그 상대가 허락이나 요청을 받아 들이는 게 됩니다.

	Questions (의문)	Answers (답)	
허락 요청	Do you mind if I 현재? Would you mind if I 과거? 해도 괜찮을까요?	No, I don't/wouldn't mind. Not at all.	Yes, I do/would.
부탁	Do/Would you mind -ing? 해줄 수 있어요? 해줄래요?	네, 괜찮아요.	아니요. 괜찮지 않아 요.

비록 같은 의미이지만, 맞는 시제의 단어를 꼭 사용해주세요.
<u>Do</u> you mind if I <u>현재(동사)</u>?
<u>Would</u> you mind if I <u>과거(동사)</u>?

이렇게 만듭니다!

표현에 따라 알맞은 형태의 동사를 붙여요.

Questions (의문)
이거 해도 괜찮을까요? **Do you mind if I do this?** **Would you mind if I did this?**
이거 해 주실 수 있으세요? **Do you mind doing this?** **Would you mind doing this?**

<유용한 표현 >

'I don't mind - ing' 난 괜찮아, 상관없어.
난 여기에 있어도 상관없어 (=괜찮아).
I don't mind staying here.

Do you mind if I ?

☞ 오른쪽 힌트를 이용해서, 직접 문장을 만들어보세요!

훈련용 MP3

정답확인 : P 329

01	제가 여기 앉아도 괜찮겠어요? 앉을데가 (아무데도) 없네요. 🔊	
02	이거 가져가도 괜찮겠어요? 🔊	
03	제가 그 애한테 말해도 괜찮겠어요? 그 애도 알아야 해요. 🔊	
04	제가 그거 봐도 될까요? 제 눈으로 직접 봐야겠어요. 🔊	눈으로 직접 with one's own eyes
05	개인적인 질문 하나 해도 괜찮을까요? 제가 오랫동안 이 질문을 한다는 게⋯ 제 질문을 할 좋은 기회예요.	
06	이거 좀 열어 놔도 괜찮겠어요? 🔊	열어 놓다 leave-open
07	이따가 제가 다시 전화해도 괜찮겠어요? 제가 지금 뭔 가 (하는) 중이라서요. 🔊	뭔가 (하는) 중 in the middle of something
08	스케줄 재조정해도 괜찮겠어요? 🔊	
09	이거 내일 돌려줘도 괜찮겠어요? 🔊	돌려주다 give-back/ return
10	내일 알려드려도 괜찮을까요? 아직 결정을 안 했어요. 🔊	

Do you mind if I ?

☞ 오른쪽 힌트를 이용해서, 직접 문장을 만들어보세요!

11	제가 5분 있다가 다시 와도 될까요? 금방 돌아올게요.	
12	이걸로 골라도 괜찮을까요?	
13	제가 이거 열어 봐도 될까요? 이 안에 뭐가 있는지 알고싶어요.	
14	제가 이걸 저기에 놓아도 괜찮을까요?	
15	제가 같이 해도(합석) 될까요?	같이하다, 합석하다 join
16	내가 너랑 같이 가도 괜찮을까?	
17	제가 지금 가도 될까요? 괜찮지요(, 그렇죠)?	괜찮다, 신경이 안쓰인다 don't mind
18	제가 이거 가지고 있어도 괜찮을까요? 나중에 필요할지도 몰라서요.	
19	너한테 내일 갚아도 될까?	갚다 pay-back
20	이거 다시 해도 괜찮을까요?	다시 하다 redo

Do you mind if I ?

☞ 오른쪽 힌트를 이용해서, 직접 문장을 만들어보세요!

21	제가 가족하고 먼저 상의해봐도 괜찮을까요? 가족하고 상의한 후에, 결정하고 싶어요.	상의하다 talk to
22	제가 생각해봐도 괜찮겠어요? 지금 당장은 결정 못 하 겠어요. 생각할 시간이 필요해요.	
23	제가 얘랑 잠깐만 얘기해도 괜찮을까요? 오래 안 걸릴 거예요.	
24	제가 잠깐만 누워도 괜찮을까요? 어지러워요.	눕다 lie down 어지럽다 feel dizzy
25	이거 집에 가져가도 괜찮을까요?	
26	제가 잠깐 한국말 좀 해도 괜찮을까요? 제 친구가 영어를 안 해서요. 얘한테 이걸 설명해주고 싶어요.	설명하다 explain-to
27	한 모금 마셔도 괜찮을까요?	한모금 마시다 take/have a sip
28	이따가 이거 픽업하러 다시 와도 괜찮을까요?	
29	나 이 샌드위치 먹어도 괜찮을까요? 하루종일 아무것도 안 먹었어. 좀 먹을래요?	
30	이 전화 좀 받아도 괜찮을까요? 이 전화 기다리고 있었어요.	이 전화 받다 take this call

Would you mind if I ?

☞ 오른쪽 힌트를 이용해서, 직접 문장을 만들어보세요!

31	너의 전화 좀 써도 괜찮을까요? 제 전화가 죽었어요.	죽은 (배터리 없는) dead
32	제가 오늘 5분 일찍 나가도 괜찮을까요?	
33	제가 뭔가 말해도 될까요?	
34	한 번 둘러봐도 될까요?	한 번 둘러보다 (take a) look around
35	이 의자 가져가도 괜찮으시겠어요? 이거 쓰는 건가요?	
36	그거 내일 찾으러 가도 괜찮을까요? 오늘은 제가 시간이 없어요.	
37	그거 내일 모레 가져다 드려도 괜찮을까요?	내일 모레 the day after tomorrow
38	제가 조금 늦게 와도 괜찮을까요? 조금 늦을지도 몰라서요.	
39	이거 맛 봐도 될까요? 맛있어 보여요. 냄새도 맛있어요.	맛보다 taste 냄새나다 smell
40	제가 그걸 적어도 괜찮을까요?	적다 write (-down)

Would you mind if I ?

41	이거 해봐도 괜찮을까요?	
42	이거 복사 좀 해도 괜찮을까요?	복사하다 copy
43	이거 나중에 해도 괜찮을까요? 지금은 제가 시간이 없어서요. 제가 할 수 있는대로, 할게요.	
44	제가 이거 켜 놔도 괜찮을까요?	켜 놓다 leave-on
45	천천히 해도 될까요? 서두르고 싶지 않아요.	천천히 하다 take one's time
46	제가 이거 섞어도 괜찮을까요?	
47	이거 닫아도 괜찮을까요?	
48	제 친구를 초대해도 괜찮을까요?	
49	저희 이거에 대해선 나중에 논의해도 괜찮을까요?	논의하다, 얘기하다 talk about
50	제가 이 사진 올려도 괜찮으시겠어요?	올리다, 게시하다 post/upload

Do you mind -ing?

☞ 오른쪽 힌트를 이용해서, 직접 문장을 만들어보세요!

51	그거 다시 확인해줄래요?	
52	이거 해주실 수 있으세요?	
53	제 아이패드에 문제가 있는데요, 좀 봐주실 수 있어요?	문제 a problem with 보다 take/have a look at
54	차에 문제가 있는데요, 도와줄래요?	
55	저한테 보여주실래요?	
56	기다려 줄래요? 금방 돌아올게요.	
57	거기 가는 길에 날 데리러 와줄 수 있으세요?	가는길 on the/one's way
58	제 가방좀 잠시 봐주실 수 있으세요?	보다. 감시하다 watch
59	요리 법을 나눠 주실 수 있어요?	요리 법 the recipe
60	어제 거기에 스카프 두고왔어요. 찾아 봐줄 수 있어요?	

61	그것 좀 줄여 줄 수 있으세요?	줄이다 turn-down
62	이거 반으로 잘라 줄 수 있으시겠어요?	반으로 in half
63	다음번엔 오시기 전에 먼저 전화 해줄 수 있어요?	
64	이거 왜 아직 안 한건지 나한테 말해 줄 수 있을까요?	
65	그거 닫아 놔 줄 수 있어요?	닫아 놓다 leave-closed
66	저 이것 좀 도와주실 수 있을까요?	도와주다 help-with
67	여기 잠깐만 멈춰주실 수 있을까요?	
68	그걸 제게 설명해 주실 수 있으시겠어요?	설명하다 explain-to
69	저것 좀 받아줄 수 있어요?	(전화, 벨 등) 받다 get
70	대답해 줄 수 있어요?	

71	이거 프린트 좀 해주실 수 있을까요?	프린트 하다 print
72	이걸 먼저 해줄 수 있을까요?	
73	그것 좀 꺼줄래요?	끄다 turn/switch-off
74	제게 리모콘 좀 건네줄래요?	건네주다 hand 리모콘 the remote (control)
75	너의 짐을 지금 싸줄래요? 우리 내일 떠날거잖아요. 지금 짐 싸는 게 좋을 것 같아요.	짐싸다 pack one's bag
76	짐 방에서 풀어줄래요?	짐풀다 unpack one's bag
77	짐 싣는 것 좀 도와줄 수 있어요?	짐 싣다 load
78	짐 내리는 것 좀 도와줄 수 있어요?	짐 내리다 unload
79	이것 좀 잡고 있어줄래요?	잡다, 잡고 있다 hold
80	조금만 천천히 가줄래요?	천천히 가다 slow down

Would you mind -ing?

☞ 오른쪽 힌트를 이용해서, 직접 문장을 만들어보세요!

81	그것 좀 닦아 줄 수 있으세요?	닦다 wipe
82	차 좀 빼줄 수 있을까요?	빼다, 움직이다 move
83	제게 시간을 더 주실래요?	
84	더 가까이 와줄래요?	더 가까이 closer
85	눈 감아 줄 수 있어요?	눈을 감다 close one's eyes
86	내 이마 좀 만져봐 줄래요? (저) 열 있어요?	만지다, 느끼다 feel 이마 forhead 열 나다 have a fever
87	그 얼룩 좀 지워줄 수 있을까요?	지우다 remove 얼룩 the stain
88	제 옆에 앉아 줄래요? 지금은 혼자이고 싶지 않아.	옆에 next to
89	저녁 거의 다 되었어. 숟가락 놓아줄래요?	숟가락 등을 놓다 set the table
90	그것 좀 여기에 적어주실 수 있을까요? 그게 무슨 뜻인지 모르겠어요.	

91	난 기다리는 거 괜찮아. 천천히 해요.	천천히 하다 take one's time
92	여기 서있는 거 괜찮아요. 전 걱정하지 마세요.	
93	전 혼자 가는 것 괜찮아요. 같이 가지 않아도 돼요.	같이 가다 come along
94	여기서 먹어도 괜찮아. 너가 여기서 먹고 싶으면, 우리 그래도 돼.	
95	전 여기 앉아도 상관없어요.	
96	전 그 애 돕는 거 괜찮아요. 그 앤 우리의 도움이 필요하잖아요.	
97	이거 하는 거 전 상관없어요. 이거 하는 거 좋아해요. 돕는 게 기뻐요.	
98	너가 지금 운전하고 싶지 않으면, 내가 운전해도 상관없어.	
99	나 여기 있어도 상관없어. 하지만, 너가 다른 곳에 가고 싶다면, 그래도 돼.	다른 곳 somewhere else
100	난 소파에서 자도 괜찮아. 내가 여기 있게 해줘서 고마워.	있게 하다/허락하다 let-stay

Positive (긍정)	Negative (부정)	Question (의문)
Do/Go ····. [동사 바로]	**Don't**	-
해, 하세요	하지 마, 하지 마세요	-
I used to	**I didn't use to**	**Did you use to?**
옛날엔 했었는데··· (지금은 안 해)	옛날엔 안 했었는데··· (지금은 해)	옛날엔 했었어?
I was going to	**I wasn't going to**	**Were you going to?**
하려고 했었는데··· (안 했어)	안 하려고 했었는데··· (했어)	하려고 했었어?
There is	**There isn't**	**Is there?**
있어	없어	있어?
There was	**There wasn't**	**Was there?**
있었어	없었어	있었어?
There will be	**There won't be**	**Will there be?**
있을 거야	없을 거야	있을까?
I have been -ing	**I haven't been -ing**	**Have you been -ing?**
하고 있었어 (지금)	안 하고 있었어	하고 있었어?

Questions (의문)	Answers (답)	
Do you mind if I 현재? Would you mind if I 과거?	No, I don't/ wouldn't mind. Not at all.	Yes, I do/would.
해도 괜찮을까요?		
Do/Would you mind -ing?	네, 괜찮아요	아니요.
해줄 수 있어요? 해줄래요?		

01	내가 찾아볼 게. 찾으면, 바로 전화할 게. [바로 right away]
02	우리 그거 찾아봐야 돼.
03	너 지금 뭔가 찾고 있지 (, 그렇지)? 뭐야?
04	집에 가면, 널 위해 찾아볼 수 있어.
05	어제 집에 와서 찾아보려고 했었는데. 깜빡했어.
06	그 애가 널 찾을 수도 있어.
07	난 그거 지금 찾아보고 싶어.
08	아침내내 내 흰 가방 찾고 있어. 봤어?
09	나라면, 해결책을 찾아볼 거야.
10	우리 같이 찾아보는 게 좋겠어.
11	난 그거 다 찾아봤어. [다 everywhere] 하지만 못 찾았어. 잃어버렸어.
12	나 이거 찾고 있던건데, 고마워. 어디서 찾았니?
13	여기 너무 많은 것들이 있어. 여기선 그거 못 찾아 보겠어.
14	우리 그거 안 찾아봐도 돼. 필요없어.
15	나 아무것도 찾고 있지 않아.

정답확인 : P 334

16	내가 거기 찾아봤나 생각이 안 나.
17	난 그거 다시는 안 찾아볼 거야.
18	난 그거 어젯밤에 못 찾아봤어. 미안.
19	그거 찾아보고 싶지 않아. **시간낭비야.** [시간낭비 a waste of time]
20	그 애 나 안 찾았지 (, 그렇지)?
21	넌 날 다신 안 찾는 게 좋겠어.
22	나 찾지 마.
23	너 그거 찾아 볼거야? 언제 할 거야?
24	우리 어디 찾아보는게 좋을까?
25	찾고 있는 게 (뭔가) 있어요?
26	우리 같이 찾아볼까?
27	거기에 그거 두고 왔어. 그거 찾아 봐줄래?
28	너 뭘 찾고 있는지 말해줄래?
29	찾아 봤어?
30	제가 찾아봐도 되나요?

31	너 뭔가 찾고 있었어?
32	제가 그걸 찾아봐도 괜찮을까요?
33	그거 찾아봐야 하나요? 그거 있어야 하나요?
34	그건 마치 서울에서 김 서방이야. [마치 ~한 like]
35	그건 마치 서울에서 김 서방 찾기였어. 불가능 했어.
36	우린 서울에서 김 서방을 찾고 있어.

입국심사

A: Could you get your passport, arrival card and customs form ready? What's the purpose of your visit/trip? [Business or pleasure?]

B: I'm here on business.

I'm here for vacation.

I'm here to attend an international food conference.

I'm here to study.

A: What's your nationality?

B: I'm Korean.

A: North or south?

B: I'm from South Korea.

A: What's your occupation/profession?

B: Sorry, I didn't catch that. Could you repeat the question?

-

A: Where do you plan to stay? Where are you going to stay? /Where will you be staying?

B: I'm going to stay at Four Seasons.

A: What's the address of the hotel?

B: The address of the hotel is here.

A: Have you ever been here before? Is this your first visit?

B: I have never been here before. This is my first visit.

A: Do you have any family or relatives here?

B: No, I don't have any family or relatives here.

A: How long do you plan/intend to stay? (/How long are you here for?)

B: I am going to stay here for 10 days.

A: Do you have a return ticket?

B: Here is my itinerary. I have booked a return ticket.

입국심사

A: 당신의 여권, 도착카드[arrival card]와 세관신고서[customs form]

를 준비해주시겠어요? 당신의 방문(의) 목적이 무엇입니까?

[Business or pleasure?]

B: 사업 차(on) 왔습니다. [~하러 온 here]

휴가를 위해 왔습니다.

국제 음식 컨퍼런스에 참가하러 왔습니다.

공부하러 왔습니다.

A: 당신의 국적[nationality]은 무엇입니까?

B: 한국인입니다.

A: 북이요 남이요?

B: 남한에서 왔습니다.

A: 당신의 직업[occupation/profession]이 무엇입니까?

B: 죄송합니다. 못 들었습니다. [알아듣다 catch] 질문을 다시 해주

시겠어요? [다시 하다 repeat]

-

A: 어디에서 머무를 계획입니까?

B: 포시즌스에서 머무를 거예요.

A: 호텔의 주소가 무엇입니까?

B: 호텔 주소는 여기 있어요.

A: 여기 전에 와본 적 있습니까? 이번이 첫 방문입니까?

B: 여기 전에 와본 적 없습니다. 이게 제 첫 방문입니다.

A: 여기 가족이나 친척이 있어요?

B: 가족이나 친척이 여기에 없습니다.

A: 얼마나 오래 머무를 계획입니까?

B: 10일 있을 겁니다.

A: 돌아가는 항공권이 있습니까?

B: 여기 제 일정표입니다. 왕복 티켓 예약했습니다.

입국심사

When are you going to go back to your country?

Do you plan to work during your stay?

Are you going to work while you are here?

How many bags do you have?

How much money are you bringing?

How much money do you have? Are you bringing more than 10,000 us dollars?

Do you have anything to declare?

-

Please look into the camera.

Can you face(/turn to) the camera, please?

Place your thumb on the fingerprint reader, please.

Please place your right hand on the scanner.

Thank you. Enjoy your stay.

_____ **입국심사**

당신의 나라로 언제 돌아가실 겁니까?

당신의 방문(stay) 동안 일 할 계획입니까?

당신이 여기 있는 동안에 일 할 거예요?

몇 개의 가방을 가지고 계세요?

얼마의 돈을 가지고 오시는 겁니까?

얼마를 가지고 계십니까? 미화로 만 불 보다 더 가지고 오시나요?

세관 신고할 것을 (아무것이라도) 가지고 계십니까?

-

카메라를 보세요. [보다 look into]

카메라로 얼굴을 돌려 주시겠어요? [얼굴 돌리다 face/turn to]

지문인식기 [the fingerprint reader] 위에 엄지손가락을 놓아주세요.

[놓다 place]

스캐너위에 오른손을 놓아주세요.

감사합니다. 당신의 방문(stay)을 즐기세요.

정/답/체/크

Unit 1

1. Buy this/this one/it. It's a good price.

2. Put it/this on. It/This looks good/nice on you.

3. Try it/that. You are going to (/will) like it. I'm sure.

4. Try some/it. Otherwise you are going to (/will) get hungry later.

5. Finish it/that/this.

6. Think about it/that/this.

7. When you decide, (please) let me know.

8. Drive safely. When you get/arrive home, call me.

9. Before you enter/go in, (please) take your shoes off (/take off your shoes).

   And you have to take your hat off (/take off your hat).

10. Choose/Pick one. Which one do you like?

11. Please reconsider. It/This might/may be a good opportunity/chance.

12. Decide/Make a decision by Friday, and let me know.

13. Choose/Pick wisely.

14. Keep the change.

15. Believe/Trust me. This/It is going to work (out). (/ It will work (out).)

16. (Please) Forgive me. I didn't mean to hurt you.

17. Do this/it. It's your turn.

18. Have it/this. I am giving it (to you) as a gift.

19. Keep going.

20. Stop thinking about it/that.

21. Just leave it.

22. Leave me alone. I want to (/I'd like to) be alone now.

23. Feel this/it. It feels so/very/really soft./It's soft.

24. Tell me everything. I want to know. I want to (/I'd like to) hear it from you.

25. Say something. Why are you so quiet? (/ Why are you quiet like this?)

26. Until I come, stay here.

27. (Please) Turn it/that off. I don't want to (/I wouldn't like to) listen to the news now.

28. Pick it/that up. Why did you drop it?

29. Have a good/nice day.

30. Have a safe trip.

31. Watch/Look out!

32. Stop (there)!

33. (Please) Turn left here.

34. (Please) Avoid these areas/places.

35. Take this medicine/pill 3 times a day.

36. Close your eyes, and imagine.

37. Calm down. Take a deep breath.

38. When you have time, stop/drop by.

39. Install this file / these files, and restart the computer.

40. Get over it/that.

41. Be strong. You can do it!

42. (Please) Be quiet.

43. Ouch! Be gentle.

44. Be careful. When it's over, call me (/give me a ring).

45. Be a better person.

46. Be positive. You are always positive. Why are you (being) negative about this/it?

47. Be happy.

48. Just be yourself.

49. Be nice to your friend. Be kind to each other.

50. Be my love for good/forever.

51. Don't do anything before I get here/come.

52. Don't use it/this.

53. Don't move. Keep/Stay still.

54. Don't panic.

55. Don't go anywhere. You might/may get lost.

56. Don't worry. Everything is going to (/will) be ok. It/This is nothing.

57. Don't do it/this. I don't think you should do it/that.

58. Don't say anything.

59. Don't tell him/her. He/She will be upset.

60. Don't wait for me. I think I'll be late tonight.

61. If you aren't sure about it, don't do it yet.

62. Don't overdo it. I wouldn't overdo it.

63. Don't give it/that up. Never (ever) give up. Your dream(s) will (/is(are) going to) come true.

64. Don't cry. Please stop crying. I am going to (/will) cry, too.

65. Don't feed the animals here.

66. Don't swim here.

67. Don't use (the) electronic devices here.

68. If you need help, don't hesitate. You can contact/call me anytime.

69. Don't feel bad about it/that. It's ok.

70. If you don't want to do it, don't (do it). I am ok with it.

71. Don't laugh. I'm serious.

72. Don't overreact.

73. Don't change the subject. What's your answer?

74. Don't touch anything.

75. Don't eat it/that. It's spoiled/rotten.

76. Don't drink it/that. I/We/You have to check the expiration date.

77. Don't forget your belongings.

78. Don't forget to bring this card.

79. Don't do anything. You don't have to do everything.

80. Don't talk/speak to me like that.

81. Don't complain.

82. Don't yell (/scream/shout) at me. I am not deaf.

83. Don't just stand there! Do something.

84. Don't tell me what to do. When I'm ready, I will do it.

85. Don't get angry/mad. If you promise, I will tell you.

86. Don't blame yourself. It's nobody's/no one's fault. (/It isn't anybody's/anyone's fault.)

87. Don't be surprised/shocked.

88. Don't make fun of others/other people.

89. Don't think like that. It's not good.

90. Don't think about your weakness. Your weakness can be/become your strength.

91. Don't be afraid.

92. Don't be scared.

93. Don't be silly.

94. Don't be late.

95. Don't be sick. Especially when I am not here (with you)/around.

96. Don't be nervous. You are ready!

97. Don't be greedy.

98. Don't be sad. When you are sad, I'm sad too.

99. Don't be nice to him/her. He/She is mean.

100. Don't be hard on yourself. You are doing well!

Review

1. You can sit here.

2. I think we should sit there.

3. I have to sit here. I want to (/I'd like to) sit here.

4. I will sit here with you.

5. I'm going to sit with a/my friend (over) there. See you later.

6. Somebody/Someone is sitting here.

7. He /She always sits with me. I have to save this seat (for him/her). He / She will be here/come soon.

8. When I went there, someone/somebody was sitting there.

9. I just sat there. (/I was just sitting there.) I didn't know what to say.

10. (Please) Sit here.

11. He/She might/may sit here. He/She usually sits here.

12. I would sit there. It's a good spot/seat.

13. We can sit together.

14. It's nice/good to sit with you.

15. We might as well sit here.

16. I don't think we should sit together today.(/We shouldn't sit together today.)

17. I don't think I'll sit with him/her.

18. I'm not going to sit there today. I don't like that/the seat.

19. Don't sit there. It's wet.

20. I might/may not sit with my friend. I don't think my friend/he/she will come today.

21. We don't have to sit here. If you don't want (to).

22. I don't think he/she will sit alone.

23. I am not sitting here. You can take it. I'm sitting there.

24. He/She doesn't sit alone. He/She is always with (his/her) friends. He/

She has many (/a lot of) friends.

25. I didn't sit alone.

26. I couldn't sit with him. He came late.

27. I don't want to (/wouldn't like to) sit here.

28. Can/Could/May I sit here?

29. Where do you want to (/would you like to) sit?

30. Can/Could/Would you sit here with me? I want to (/I'd like to) talk/speak to/with you.

31. Do we have to sit here?

32. Should we sit here?

33. Where are you sitting? Where's your seat?

34. Have you sat there?

35. Where did you sit?

36. Where does Tim sit? Where's his seat?

37. Where can we sit? Can we sit together?

38. Where shall we sit?

39. Where would you sit?

40. Where are you going to sit?

41. I want to sit this one out. I don't think I'll have time to do it/this.

42. I'm going to sit this (one) out (this time).

43. If you're tired, you can sit this one out.

44. I have to sit this one out.

Unit 2

1. I used to have long hair.

2. He/She used to have short hair.

3. He/She used to drink a lot.

4. He/She used to smoke a lot. He/She quit/stopped smoking 5 years ago.

5. I used to go there often. (/ I often used to go there.) I haven't been there for a long time.

6. We used to come here often. (/ We often used to come here.) It used to be (/ was) our favorite spot/place.

7. I never used to drink milk.

8. I used to eat this/it often. (/ I often used to eat this/it.) I don't like it now.

9. I never used to study hard. I like/love studying.

10. Jim never used to eat vegetables. He likes vegetables now.

11. When I was little/a child/a kid, I used to like this/it a lot/very much. I wanted to do it every day.

12. I used to drink a lot of coffee (/coffee a lot). I prefer tea now.

13. Mark used to work at the airport, but he drives a truck now.

14. I used to have it/that, too. (But) I lost it a few years ago. When I lost it/ that, I couldn't (even) sleep.

15. I used to work here. I work in Gangnam now.

16. I used to hate him, too. I used to misunderstand him. (/ I misunderstood him.)

17. We used to live in Gangnam. We live in Ilsan now. We moved last year.

18. We used to go to the cinema often. (/ We often used to go to the cinema.)

19. We used to work together. He used to be/was my colleague/coworker.

20. I used to travel a lot. I haven't had time to travel recently.

21. When we were little/kids/children, my brother/sister and I I used to fight all the time.

22. You used to call me every day. You (have) changed a lot.

23. You used to like it/this. Am I wrong?

24. I used to do that a lot. I used to like/love doing it/that. (/ I loved/liked

doing it/that.)

25. I used to believe/trust him/her. I don't believe/trust him/her anymore.

26. He used to look good/cool/nice. He used to be (/was) very handsome/ good looking.

27. I used to listen to this song every day. It used to be (/was) my favorite song (back) then.

28. We used to talk to each other every day.

29. I used to believe that/it, too.

30. Many people used to see it/that. It's different now.

31. We used to see each other every day. I haven't seen you for a long time. How have you been?

32. I used to collect this/it.

33. I used to spend a lot of money on it/here.

34. Parents used to do everything for their children.

35. Many people used to spend time with their family.

36. Everybody/Everyone used to want to have it/this. It used to be (/was) popular. I wanted to have it, too.

37. Everybody/Everyone used to have it/this, except me.

38. It used to take really/very/so/too long. It felt like forever.

39. It used to cost nothing. (/ It didn't use to cost anything.)

40. So many people used to be poor.

41. When I was a student, I used to be very/really/so shy.

42. When he/she was little/a kid/a child, he/she used to be outgoing.

43. Kate used to be a teacher.

44. I used to be good at it/this.

45. We used to be close to each other. Where has the time gone? (/ Where did the time go?)

46. You used to be on my side. Be on my side!

47. He/She used to be my best friend. We used to be best/really good friends.

48. Money used to be very/so/really important to me. It's still important, but it's not everything.

49. It used to be crowded. It's quiet today.

50. It used to be good/nice. It feels different now.

51. It used to be very/so/really expensive.

52. It used to be here.

53. It used to be a school. It is a hospital now.

54. It used to be my favorite.

55. It used to be very/so/really big.

56. It used to be popular.

57. It used to be there.

58. It used to be dangerous. But it is not (dangerous) now.

59. It used to be a problem. But it's not a problem now.

60. It used to be mine. I gave it to my brother/sister.

61. I didn't use to live here. I used to live alone. (/ I lived alone.)

62. I didn't use to work with him/her.

63. I didn't use to eat seafood. But I can eat it now.

64. We didn't use to like each other. We are good friends now.

65. He didn't use to cry. (But) He cries a lot now.

66. We didn't use to come here often. But we come here every Monday.

67. I didn't use to use it. Honestly (/Frankly/To be honest/To be frank), I couldn't use it. I didn't know how to use it.

68. He didn't use to tell me anything. He wants to tell me everything now. He became (/has become) chatty/talkative.

69. You didn't use to have it. When did you buy/get it?

70. I didn't use to have long hair. My hair is long now.

71. People didn't use to know about this/it.

72. You didn't use to smile much/often. It's good/nice to see your smile.

73. It didn't use to cost much/a lot. I miss those days.

74. It didn't use to take this long. It's weird/strange.

75. He didn't use to be selfish. He used to be (/was) thoughtful/considerate.

76. It didn't use to be here.

77. It didn't use to be this expensive (/expensive like this). The price has gone up (/went up).

78. When I was a student, I didn't use to be confident.

79. It didn't use to be like this. It (has) changed a lot/so much.

80. It didn't use to be hard. When did it get/become so/this hard?

81. Where did you use to live?

82. Who did you use to live with? Did you (use to) live alone?

83. Did you use to like it/this? You have (so) many of them.

84. Did you use to collect this/it? How long have you collected it/this?

85. Where did you use to work? How long did you (use to) work there?

86. When you were little/a kid/a child, what did you use to like?

87. How often did you use to come here?

88. Did he/she use to travel a lot?

89. When you were a student, did you use to wear a school uniform?

90. When you were (feeling) down, what did you use to do?

91. Did it use to take a week to go/get there? It took so/very/too long. (/It used to take so long.)

92. How long did it use to take?

93. How much did it use to cost?

94. Did it use to work? It's not easy now.

95. Did it use to be your dream?

96. Did it use to be free? That/It was good.

97. Did it use to be 5 percent? It's 10 percent now.

98. Did the price use to be lower?

99. Did it use to be slow? I can't imagine (it/that).

100. Where did it use to be?

Review

1. I think I'll cry. It's hard/difficult to say goodbye.

2. I want to (/I'd like to) cry. Everything is a mess.

3. I can cry right now. Do you want to (/Would you like to) bet?

4. I wanted to cry, but I couldn't (cry).

5. He/She is crying. Talk to him/her.

6. I might/may cry, too. Stop crying.

7. He cries a lot. He is a crybaby.

8. When you left, I cried a lot. I cried like a baby.

9. Don't cry. I'm going to cry, too. (/ I'll cry, too.)

10. I will stop crying.

11. When I saw him/her, he/she was crying.

12. I would cry, too. Sometimes, crying helps. (/Crying sometimes helps.)

13. If you want to cry, cry. After you cry, you will feel better.

14. He/She used to cry a lot. He used to be a crybaby.

15. I couldn't stop crying.

16. I didn't want to cry. (But) It/I was so/very/really sad.

17. I am not going to cry at work.

18. I don't want to cry in front of people.

19. I'm not crying. I'm ok/fine.

20. I don't cry at work.

21. I haven't cried at work before. (/ I've never cried at work.)

22. Everyone/Everybody was crying except him/her.

23. I didn't use to cry much.

24. I shouldn't cry now. It's not professional.

25. The/That movie was sad, but I didn't cry.

26. He doesn't cry much.

27. Why are you crying? Are you ok?

28. Why did you cry? Did something happen?

29. Do you want to (/Would you like to) cry?

30. Are you going to cry?

31. Were you crying?

32. I don't want to cry over spilled milk.

33. I don't think we should cry over spilled milk.

34. I don't cry over spilled milk.

35. I wouldn't cry over spilled milk.

36. I'm not going to cry over spilled milk from now (on).

37. Am I crying over spilled milk (now)?

Unit 3

1. I was going to do that/it. (I'm) Sorry.

2. I was going to call you, but I forgot.

3. I was going to do (my) homework yesterday. I didn't have time.

4. He/She was going to let you know.

5. I was going to ask him first. I didn't have a chance.

6. I was going to clean the house, and cook today. I was out all day. I don't have energy to do anything.

7. When you came, I was just going to take/have a shower.

8. We were just going to go out/leave.

9. I was going to sleep in this morning. (/ I was going to get up late this morning.) You woke me up.

10. I was going to buy it/that for you.

11. I was just going to say that, too.

12. I was going to give it/that to you anyway.

13. I was going to send it/that today. Is it too late?

14. I was going to bring it/that. (But) I forgot to bring it.

15. You were going to say something now. Go first.

16. I was going to try it/this. I don't know now.

17. You got here/came early. I was going to wait for you. How did you get here/come so fast/early?

18. I was going to wear it tonight. It's big. I (have) lost (my) weight.

19. We were just going to stay/be (at) home and watch TV.

20. I was going to take a cab/taxi.

21. I was going to pay. Thank you for the lunch.

22. I was going to turn left here.

23. I was going to order this/it. But I (have) changed my mind.

24. I was going to apologize first. Thank you for understanding.

25. I was going to choose/pick this/it. If you want it/this, have it.

26. We were just going to have dinner. Can you stay for dinner?

27. I was going to forgive him/her. He/She is mean/bad. It's hard/difficult to like him/her.

28. I was going to look that/it up. Thanks for telling me (that).

29. I was going to scold him/her. Look at his/her cute/adorable face. It always melts my anger.

30. I was going to go on a diet from today. This/It looks so/very/really delicious. I might as well begin/start from tomorrow.

31. I was going to stop him. I wanted to do that/it, but I couldn't (do it).

32. I was going to ignore that/it, too. It used to be easy to ignore (things).

33. I was going to give it/that up. But you (have) helped me a lot. I will never forget it/that. (/ I'm never going to forget it/that.)

34. Before you get here/arrive, I was going to prepare everything.

35. We were going to sign the contract. You (have) ruined it/that.

36. I was going to do it your way.

37. I was going to give it to you as a birthday gift. What do you want to (/ would you like to) have?

38. I was going to go there alone/by myself. Nobody wanted to go there. Thanks for coming/going with me.

39. I was going to let you know yesterday. (But) I haven't decided (it) yet.

40. We were going to cancel it. (But) It was non-refundable.

41. I wasn't going to go out last night. (But) I had to go somewhere.

42. I wasn't going to eat it/this. (But) It was so/very/really delicious.

43. I wasn't going to cry. (But) It was so/very/really touching/moving.

44. I wasn't going to say anything. (But) I was furious.

45. I wasn't going to bother you. Sorry. This/It is the last time.

46. I wasn't going to buy anything. (But) I (have) bought a lot of (/many) things. I (have) spent a lot (of money).

47. I wasn't going to come here (ever) again. / I was never going to come here again.

48. I wasn't going to lie, but I had no choice/I didn't have a choice.

49. I wasn't going to tell him/her. (But) He/She kept asking (me).

50. I wasn't going to say this/it. (But) He/She isn't a good person.

51. I wasn't going to give (it) up. But I couldn't keep going (/continue).

52. I wasn't going to throw it away. It was my/a mistake.

53. I wasn't going to withdraw (any) money. (But) It was cash only.

54. I wasn't going to reschedule this time. I am (so/really/very) sorry.

55. I wasn't going to think about it anymore/any longer. (But) I can't stop thinking about it.

56. He/She wasn't going to talk/speak to me. But eventually, we (have) made up.

57. I wasn't going to eat junk food. (But) Junk food tastes so/very/really good.

58. I wasn't going to see him/her (ever) again. But, he/she (has) changed a lot. If/When you see him/her, you will (/are going to) be surprised, too.

59. I wasn't going to record it/that. (But) I recorded everything. It's here.

60. I wasn't going to overdo it. When/Once I begin/start something, it's hard/difficult to stop.

61. I wasn't going to delete it/that. Can you/I restore it? (/Is it possible to restore?)

62. I wasn't going to waste my time. (But) I (have) wasted a lot of time today.

63. I wasn't going to play hard to get. (But) You started/began it first.

64. I'm sorry. I wasn't going to laugh. I am not laughing at you. I am just laughing. Ok. I will stop now.

65. I wasn't going to go anywhere this summer.

66. I wasn't going to sing. Since everybody/everyone wants it. I will sing just one song.

67. I wasn't going to expect anything.

68. I wasn't going to fight/argue/have an argument with him/her. I really tried.

69. I wasn't going to get angry/mad. But the service was terrible/awful/bad.

70. I wasn't going to break a/my promise. I'm really/so/very sorry.

71. What were you going to do there?

72. What were you going to do with it/this? Why is this/it in your pocket? (/ Why do you have it in your pocket?)

73. Were you going to go somewhere?

74. Where were you going to go?

75. When were you going to come? Were you going to come today?

76. Were you going to say something? What did you say?

77. How were you going to tell him/her?

78. Which one were you going to use? Can/Could/May I use this (one)/it?

79. What were you going to buy/get?

80. Where were you going to put/leave it/this?

81. When were you going to do it/this?

82. Were you going to tell me? When were you going to tell me?

83. How were you going to hide it/that from me? It/That is funny. I know you very/too/so/really well.

84. When were you going to fix/repair it/this?

85. Where were we going to go? I want to/I'd like to know.

86. Where were you going to take me?

87. How long were you going to stay there? What was your original plan?

88. Were you going to do it/this alone/ (all) by yourself? You have me.

89. How were you going to survive without me? You need me. Can you live

without me?

90. Were you going to return it/this? I (have) opened it.

91. Were you going to go alone/by yourself? If you want, I can come/go with you.

92. Were you going to drive there or take a train?

93. When were you going to start/begin this/it? If I were you, I would start/begin right now/away.

94. Were you going to say "yes"? You said "yes".

95. When were you going to decide? Have you made up your mind? (/Did you make up your mind?)

96. Were you going to read this book?

97. What were you going to tell me? Tell me now. I'm all ears.

98. Were you going to add this/it to cart?

99. (I'm) Sorry. Were you going to use it/this? Here it is (/Here you are).

100. Were you going to invite our boss? I wouldn't invite him/her. Please don't (invite him/her).

Review

1. Ask me anything. I'm ready.

2. I want to (/I'd like to) ask him/her something. (/ I want to ask something to him/her.)

3. I will ask him/her.

4. I have to ask you something. (/ I have to ask something to you.)

5. I think we should ask him/her first.

6. I think he/she will ask you.

7. I'm going to ask a personal question, you have to answer me.

8. It was hard/difficult to ask.

9. I'm asking you. Can/Could/Would you do it for me?

10. I wanted to ask you something (/ask something to you). (But) I forgot.

11. I asked him/her. He/She is going to (/will) help (you/us/me).

12. He asks too many questions.

13. When he/she was little, he/she used to ask many (/a lot of) questions (/ he asked many questions).

14. I was going to ask you that, too.

15. They may/might ask personal questions at the interview.

16. I would ask for help.

17. You don't have to ask every time.

18. I can't ask him/her anymore. I (have) asked too many times.

19. I don't want to (/wouldn't like to) ask him/her. He/She is not kind.

20. I didn't ask you. You just did it.

21. Don't ask. I don't want to (/wouldn't like to) think about it anymore/any longer.

22. They didn't ask me many questions at the interview. Is it/that a bad sign?

23. I don't ask (questions). I just do it/them.

24. I don't have to ask (questions). He just tells me everything.

25. I haven't asked him/her yet. When I see him/her, I will (do it/that).

26. I couldn't ask him/her. I didn't have a chance to talk to him.

27. I'm not going to ask him/her. I think he/she will say "no" anyway.

28. Can/Could/Would you ask nicely? If I were you, I would ask nicely.

29. What do you want to (/would you like to) ask me?

30. Can/Could/May I ask something?

31. What are you going to ask?

32. What were you going to ask?

33. Did you ask for help? (/Have you asked for help?)

34. Am I asking too much?

35. If you were me, what would you ask?

36. What do you think I should ask?

37. What do you think you'll ask?

38. (I'm) Sorry. It/That was my friend. What were you asking me?

39. I am going to ask you something. Can/Could/Would you do it no questions asked?

40. I did it no questions asked.

41. If you don't like this product, you can return it no questions asked.

42. I will do it no questions asked.

Unit 4

1. There is something (in) here.

2. There is something in my shoe(s).

3. There is a post office on the corner.

4. There is someone/somebody outside.

5. There is someone/somebody in front of the car.

6. There is a light on.

7. There is a (swimming) pool in/at our hotel. You can use it 24/7.

8. There is enough time.

9. There is a lot of traffic/a traffic jam.

10. There is a lot of (/too much) salt in this soup. It's salty.

11. There is a train at 10.

12. There is a plane at 11 tonight.

13. There is a bus to the airport (from) here.

14. If/When there is a problem, there is a solution, too.

15. There is a possibility.

16. There is a way.

17. There is a way to solve/fix this/it.

18. There is something to say.

19. There is something I want to tell you.

20. There is something you have to see.

21. There are a lot of (/so many/too many) people.

22. There are a lot of (/so many/too many) cars.

23. There are 3 rooms in the house.

24. There are 20 students in the/that class.

25. There are 4 people (/members) in my family.

26. There are some sandwiches on the table. Help yourself.

27. There are always two sides. You (/We/I) have to listen to the both sides.

28. There are a lot of (/many) good/nice/great books. I don't know where to begin/start.

29. There are (some) cases like that. But it's rare.

30. There are a lot of (/many) ups and downs in life.

31. When/If you think about it, there are a lot of (/many) happy moments. Life is ok. There is a hope.

32. There are a lot of (/many) ways.

33. There are a lot of (/many) ways to do this/it.

34. There are a lot of (/many) things to do. I am very/so/too/really busy today.

35. There are a lot of (/many) things to see.

36. There are a lot of (/many) things to choose. It's hard (/difficult) to choose (/pick) just(/only) one.

37. There are a lot of (/many) things to say.

38. There are a lot of (/many) things I want to say.

39. There are a lot of (/many) things we can do.

40. There are a lot of (/many) things I have to do today.

41. There was a lot of traffic/a traffic jam. It took 2 hours to get/come here.

42. There was a tiny (/small/little) problem, but I fixed/solved it. It is going to (/will) be ready by this weekend.

43. There was no answer.

44. There was an accident.

45. There was a reason. Don't ask (me) why.

46. There was a conference in 대전. I had to attend the conference.

47. When we went there, there was a long line outside. I had to wait long/for a long time.

48. There was enough time to do that/it.

49. There were a lot of (/many) students in the/that class.

50. There were 10 missed calls.

51. There isn't anything in it/there. / There is nothing in it.

52. There isn't anyone/anybody. / There is nobody/no one. Where is everyone/everybody?

53. There isn't enough time.

54. There isn't any. / There is none.

55. I'm sorry/afraid, there isn't any coffee left. / There is no coffee left. Do you want to (/Would you like to) drink/have tea?

56. There isn't (any) milk in the fridge/refrigerator. We/I ran out of milk.

57. There isn't anything to say. / There is nothing to say. I don't know what to say.

58. There isn't anything to eat. / There is nothing to eat.

59. There isn't anything to buy here. / There is nothing to buy here.

60. There isn't anywhere to go. / There is nowhere to go.

61. There wasn't anything in it/there. / There was nothing in it/there.

62. There wasn't a problem. / There was no problem. Thanks to you, it was successful.

63. I wanted to do that/it, too, but there wasn't enough time. Maybe/Perhaps next time.

64. There wasn't an issue.

65. There wasn't an option like that. /There wasn't that (kind of) option.

66. There wasn't enough room/space.

67. There wasn't anyone/anybody here. / There was nobody/no one here. I felt very/so/really lonely.

68. I found a wallet/purse on the street yesterday, but there wasn't (any) money in it.

69. There wasn't a chance to do that/it.

70. I saw him/her yesterday, but there wasn't a chance to talk(/speak) to(/with) him/her.

71. There wasn't anything to wear. / There was nothing to wear.

72. There wasn't anything to do. / There was nothing to do. It was so/very/really boring. / I was so bored.

73. I was hungry, but there wasn't anything to eat / there was nothing to eat.

74. There wasn't anything to worry (about). / There was nothing to worry (about).

75. There wasn't anything to say. / There was nothing to say.

76. There wasn't anyone/anybody to replace you. / There was nobody/no one to replace you. It will be hard/difficult to replace you.

77. There wasn't anyone/anybody to talk/speak to. / There was nobody/no one to talk/speak to.

78. It was too/so/very/really late. So, there wasn't anywhere to eat. / There was nowhere to eat.

79. There wasn't anything I wanted to do. / There was nothing I wanted to do. I just wanted to stay in(side).

80. There wasn't (any) information I needed. It was a waste of time.

81. Is there a bank near/around here?

82. Is there an accident? Why are there (so) many cars (like this)?

83. Is there hot water?

84. Is there a prize? If there is a prize, I want to (/I'd like to) participate, too.

85. Is there (any) information about that/it? Where can I find it?

86. Is there only one (right/correct) answer?

87. Is there something to eat at home? Before we go home, shall we eat something?

88. Is there somewhere to go?

89. Is there something I can do? I want to (/I'd like to) help (you).

90. Are there a lot of (/many) volunteers? How many people are there?

91. Was there a mistake? Did I make a mistake? (I'm) Sorry, I will correct it.

92. Was there a lot of traffic/a traffic jam?

93. Was there a witness? Can you prove it/that?

94. Was there a blackout last night?

95. Was there a reason? What was the reason?

96. Was there a problem with the shipping/delivery?

97. Was there someone/somebody to talk/speak to?

98. Was there anything you wanted to buy? Did you buy something/anything?

99. Were there a lot of (/many) patients? Were there a lot of (/many) sick people?

100.Were there many people? How many people were there?

Review

1. I want to (/I'd like to) cook at home. Stay for dinner.

2. I can cook. I'm a good cook. / I'm good at cooking.

3. You should cook. I can't cook. / I'm not a good cook. / I'm not good at cooking.

4. I am going to cook dinner for him/her.

5. It's easy to cook.

6. I'm cooking something now. I'll call you back in 5 minutes.

7. I will cook for you.

8. He/She cooks every day.

9. When you came, I was cooking.

10. I have cooked this/it. I know how to do it.

11. We might/may cook together.

12. We might as well cook it/this at home.

13. I cooked this/it yesterday. I'll heat it up.

14. I was going to cook. Thank you.

15. (My) Mom used to cook every day. But she doesn't do that often/much.

16. There is time to cook. / We (/I) have time to cook. It's only 5.

17. It was easy to cook.

18. I shouldn't cook. Nobody is going to (/will) eat it.

19. You don't have to cook if you don't want (to). We can go out.

20. I don't want to (/wouldn't like to) cook tonight. Shall we order something?

21. I couldn't cook. There wasn't time. / I didn't have time.

22. He/She doesn't cook.

23. Don't overcook (the) vegetables.

24. I wasn't going to overcook this/it.

25. I didn't cook this/it. I bought it.

26. He/She has never cooked before. / He/she hasn't cooked before.

27. There wasn't time to cook. / I didn't have time to cook.

28. There isn't anything to cook. There is nothing to cook.

29. What shall we cook?

30. What should we cook?

31. What did you cook?

32. What are you going to cook?

33. Could/Can/Would you cook dinner today? I am going to (/will) be late.

34. What do you want to (/would you like to) cook?

35. Do you cook? Do you know how to cook this/it?

36. When we were little/children/kids, what did mom (use to) cook?

37. What are you cooking? Something smells good/nice/delicious.

38. Do I have to cook? Is it my turn?

39. Is there time to cook? / Do you have time to cook?

40. It's (just) like out of the frying pan into the fire.

41. It was (just) like out of the frying pan into the fire.

42. I jumped (/went) out of the frying pan into the fire.

Unit 5

1. There used to be a lot of (/many) people. People were (/used to be) everywhere.

2. There will/are going to be a lot of (/many) people.

3. There may/might be a lot of (/many) people.

4. There has to be someone/somebody to contact/call. Is he/she alone?

5. There may/might be a lot of (/many) people like us.

6. There will (/are going to) be a lot of (/many) victims like him/her.

7. I think there will be a lot of traffic/a traffic jam. We should go/leave early.

8. There may/might be a lot of traffic/a traffic jam.

9. There used to be a lot of traffic/a traffic jam.

10. When I go back to work from this vacation/holiday, there will (/are going to) be a lot of (/many) emails and messages.

11. There might/may be a problem. If there is a problem, let me know.

12. There have been a lot of (/many) problems. There isn't anyone/anybody (/There is nobody/no one) to solve/fix it, and/so it's a huge problem.

13. There used to be a lot of (/many) problems.

14. I think there will be a problem.

15. There has to be a solution to this problem.

16. There used to be a lot of free time. It used to be (/ It was) good.

17. There might/may be enough time.

18. There will (/is going to) be time to go to the bathroom/toilet.

19. There will (/is going to) be time to ask questions after the speech.

20. There has to be time for ourselves.

21. There may/might be a test.

22. There will be final exams/tests next week.

23. There have been a lot of (/many) tests/exams this month.

24. There has to be a test.

25. There will (/is going to) be another chance. It's ok.

26. There may/might be another chance soon. Who knows?

27. There has to be another chance. I'll do better next time.

28. There will (/are going to) be a lot of (/many) chances/opportunities.

29. There have been many chances. It's not late yet.

30. There might/may be a seminar next weekend.

31. There have been many changes. Everything has changed.

32. There will (/is going to) be a change at our school. There will (/are going to) be new teachers.

33. There has to be a big change.

34. There may/might be a change in our plan. If it/that happens, I'll let you know.

35. There will (/is going to) be a way. There's always a way.

36. There may/might be a way. When one door closes, another door opens. It's always like that.

37. There has to be a way.

38. I think there will a better way.

39. There has to be a better way.

40. There will (/are going to) be a lot of (/many) ways to fix/solve that/it.

41. There will (/are going to) be a lot of (/many) benefits.

42. There has to be a benefit. Otherwise, what's the point/use?

43. There may/might be a lot of (/many) temptations. I want to (/I'd like to) be strong.

44. There will (/are going to) be a lot of (/many) temptations. We have to be strong.

45. When you arrive at the airport, there will (/is going to) be someone/somebody to pick you up.

46. There will (/is going to) be a soccer match/game on TV tomorrow evening. I am going to go home early and/to watch it.

47. There will (/are going to) be a lot of (/many) new features/functions.

48. There used to be a bank here.

49. There will (/are going to) be new shops/stores and buildings here.

50. There will (/are going to) be pros and cons. I think we should consider all the pros and cons.

51. There will (/are going to) be a lot of (/many) fun activities. I would want to go.

52. There will (/are going to) be a lot of (/many) things to eat.

53. There will (/are going to) be a lot of (/many) things to learn. We learn something new every day.

54. I think there will be a lot of (/many) things to do. It will (/is going to) be fun. I'm excited. /It's exciting.

55. There will (/are going to) be a lot of (/many) things to see.

56. There will (/are going to) be a lot of (/many) places to go.

57. There will (/is going to) be everything. You don't need to bring anything.

58. There will (/is going to) be everything you need.

59. There may/might be something you need. If there is something you need (/ if you need something), come to me anytime.

60. There have been many complaints about/against our company. We need new ideas.

61. There won't (/aren't going to) be a lot of (/many) people.

62. There didn't use to be a lot of (/many) people.

63. There may/might not be a lot of (/many) people.

64. There won't (/isn't going to) be a problem. You don't need to worry.

65. There may/might not be a problem.

66. Since we changed the system, there hasn't been a problem.

67. I don't think there will be enough.

68. There may/might not be enough. Take more, just in case.

69. There may/might not be another chance.

70. There won't (/isn't going to) be the same chance. But I think there will be a better chance.

71. There won't (/aren't going to) be any conditions. Are you in?

72. There doesn't have to be a reason. There are things we can't explain.

73. I think there will be a lot of (/many) things to do tomorrow.

74. There won't (/isn't going to) be anything to worry. / There will (/is going to) be nothing to worry (about).

75. There may/might not be anything to eat at home. / There may/might be nothing to eat at home.

76. It/That is a small town. There won't (/isn't going to) be anywhere to go. / There will (/is going to) be nowhere to go.

77. There won't (/isn't going to) be anything to say. / There will (/is going to) be nothing to say.

78. There won't (/isn't going to) be anything I want to say. / There will (/is going to) be nothing I want to say.

79. There won't (/isn't going to) be anything I want to do there. / There will (/is going to) be nothing I want to do there. I don't want to (/wouldn't like to) go.

80. There may/might not be anything we can do for him. / There may/might be nothing we can do for him.

81. Will there be a way? / Is there going to be a way?

82. Will there be a solution? / Is there going to be a solution?

83. Will there be a lot of traffic/a traffic jam? / Is there going to be a lot of traffic/a traffic jam? When should we go out/leave?

84. Will there be a lot of (/many) people? / Are there going to be a lot of (/

many) people? What do you think?

85. How many people will there be (/are there going to be)?

86. Did there use to be a lot of (/many) people here?

87. Does there have to be a reason? There isn't a reason. / There is no reason.

88. Will there be free Wi-Fi? / Is there going to be free Wi-Fi?

89. Will there be a problem? / Is there going to be a problem?

90. Will there be a future between us? / Is there going to be a future between us?

91. Will there be time? / Is there going to be time?

92. Will there be time to go to/visit the museum? / Is there going to be time to go to the museum?

93. Will there be enough time? / Is there going to be enough time?

94. Do you think there will be time to finish that/it?

95. How much time will there be? / How much time is there going to be?

96. Will there be a chance? / Is there going to be a chance?

97. I (have) missed this chance. Do you think there will be another chance?

98. Will there be time to ask questions after the ceremony? / Is there going to be time to ask questions after the ceremony?

99. Will there be a possibility? / Is there going to be a possibility?

100. How much possibility will there (/is there going to) be?

Review

1. I want to (/I'd like to) see you.

2. You have to see this/it. It's so/really/very funny.

3. I'm going to see a movie this weekend.

4. I can see you this Friday.

5. It is good/nice to see you again. Have you been well?

6. I see him/her once a week.

7. I have seen it/that. / I saw it/that.

8. I have seen it/that before.

9. I might/may see him/her later.

10. I've seen it many times. / I saw it many times.

11. We used to see each other every day.

12. I was going to see him/her yesterday, but he/she was too/very/so busy. So, he cancelled (it).

13. We might as well see this movie.

14. There is something I want to see.

15. There will (/are going to) be a lot of (/many) things to see. It is going to (/will) be fun.

16. It was very/so/really nice/good to see you.

17. I don't want to (/wouldn't like to) see him/her again.

18. I'm not going to see him/her again.

19. I don't think we should see (each other) anymore.

20. I can't see you this week.

21. If you don't want, I won't see it.

22. You don't have to see him/her.

23. I haven't seen you for a long time. How have you been?

24. I don't see him much/often.

25. I haven't seen it/that yet. I'm going to see it later.

26. I didn't see him/her yesterday.

27. If I were you, I wouldn't see this movie.

28. I wasn't going to see it/this without you. There wasn't anything to do. / There was nothing to do. It was so/very/really boring. / I was so bored.

29. When I went there, I couldn't see it. It wasn't there.

30. He/She may/might not see us.

31. Can/Could/May I see it?

32. What are you going to see?

33. What do you want to (/would you like to) see?

34. What shall we see?

35. What should we see?

36. What did you see?

37. Have you seen this movie? / Did you see this movie?

38. What were you going to see?

39. Is there anything you want to see?

40. Will there be a lot of (/many) things to see? /Are there going to be a lot of (/many) things to see?

41. Were there a lot of (/many) things to see?

42. We saw eye to eye. We always see eye to eye.

43. We didn't see eye to eye.

44. My mom doesn't see eye to eye with me.

Unit 6

1. Can you tell me where you have to go now? Where are you going?

2. Tell me where you want to (/you'd like to) go. I want to (/I'd like to) know where you want to (/you'd like to) go.

3. I don't know where we will go this summer. We might/may go to Jeju Island.

4. I don't know where I should go this time. I haven't been to China yet. Have you been there?

5. I'm not sure when I can go. I'm still at work. There are a lot of/many

things to do. / I have a lot of/many things to do.

6. I want to (/I'd like to) know where you are going.

7. Tell me where you went yesterday.

8. I don't know where he/she has gone (/ he/she went). Where has he/she gone? / Where did he/she go?

9. I wonder where he/she was going.

10. I have to ask when I can go/come.

11. I don't know what I want to (/I'd like to) do. I want to (/I'd like to) know what I want and what I can do.

12. Do you know what we have to do now? What do we do now? / What should/shall we do now?

13. I want to (/I'd like to) know what I can do for you. You know how much I support you.

14. I know what you should do. You should go out more. If/When you do that, you will feel better.

15. I'm not sure what I'm going to(/will) do tomorrow. I don't have (any) plans. What are you going to do?

16. I don't know what I am doing now. Who is this/it for? Is this/it for me/myself?

17. I can't/don't remember what I did yesterday. I didn't do much (yesterday).

18. Do you know what he/she does (for a living)? He/She is an accountant.

19. Can you show me what you have done so far?

20. I wonder what he/she was doing there. He/She doesn't go there.

21. I want to (/I'd like to) know what you need.

22. I don't know what I will need.

23. Do you know what he/she wants?

24. I wonder why he/she can't (/doesn't) understand.

25. I don't know what I want to/I'd like to eat.

26. He/She said something. I forgot what he/she said.

27. Can you tell me where you are going to go, who you are going to go with, and how long you are going to stay there?

28. Can you let me know when you can deliver it/this?

29. I don't know what I did (/have done) wrong. I didn't do (/haven't done) anything wrong.

30. I don't know which one I have to use. Can you tell me which one I should use (/which one is better to use)?

31. Can you let me know what time you can come?

32. Do you know what time I have to come?

33. Can you tell me what time you finish work?

34. You don't know (/ You have no idea) how hard I tried. You will never know.

35. I don't know what he will say.

36. I know what you mean.

37. Do you know what this/it means?

38. I want to(/I'd like to) know how long you have been in Korea.

39. I know what you were going to say. You don't have to say it/that.

40. I'm not sure where we are going to meet.

41. I don't know what time it/this will begin/start. It has to start/begin soon.

42. Do you know where he/she lives? Does he/she live near/around here?

43. I wonder what time I came/got home.

44. I want to (/I'd like to) know how I can help you.

45. Can you tell me what I have to write here?

46. I don't understand why you hate him/her. He/She is really nice/ok.

47. I want to (/I'd like to) know where you are staying.

48. I don't know what you were going to do with it/that.

49. I can't (/don't) remember where I parked my car.

50. We/I have to know what we are going to buy/get.

51. I don't understand why I have to understand him/her.

52. Tell me what you want to (/you'd like to) have/get.

53. Can you tell me how long it will take?

54. I forgot how long it took.

55. I don't know how long it takes. Do you know how long it takes?

56. Do you know how long we can stay here?

57. I don't know how long we have known each other. It has been very/so/ really long. Since we were little/children/kids, we have been friends.

58. Can you tell me what it/this does?

59. I can't find my sunglasses. I forgot where I put/left them.

60. I forgot what I was going to say. How did you know what I was going to say?

61. I don't know how I used to do this/it.

62. Can you tell me what you are looking for?

63. I don't know why I did that/it. I don't know why I said that/it.

64. Tell me how long I have to wait.

65. Can you tell me how I can get/go there from here?

66. I can't (/don't) remember where I bought/got it/this.

67. I don't know when we can see each other again.

68. I want to (/I'd like to) know what you are thinking (about).

69. I want to (/I'd like to) know what you think about this/it. / I want to know what your thoughts are about this.

70. I don't know how it/that happened. Do you know when it/that

happened?

71. Can you tell me what you want to (/you'd like to) order?

72. Can you let me know how much we have to pay?

73. I don't know how I feel (/I'm feeling).

74. I don't know why I misunderstood (it/him).

75. I forgot what I was going to buy/get. I left the list at home.

76. I don't know how long I have had it/this.

77. I wonder where they are going.

78. I don't know what time I went to sleep.

79. I want to (/I'd like to) know how I can help you.

80. I don't know how I will solve/fix it/this. I wonder if/whether I can fix/ solve it.

81. I don't know if/whether I have to do it/this.

82. Tell me if/whether you can do it/this.

83. I want to(/I'd like to) know if/whether you have already done (/you already did) it/that.

84. Can you tell me if/whether you have done (/tried) it/that?

85. I don't know if/whether I should do it/that. Will it be better to do (that)? /Should I do that/it?

86. I don't know if/whether you want to (/you'd like to) do it/this.

87. I wonder if/whether I can do it/this.

88. I'm(/We're) not sure if/whether we will do it/this.

89. I wonder if/whether he/she is doing something. There is something I have to tell him/her.

90. Do you know if/whether he/she likes it/this?

91. I don't know if/whether it works (/is working). I haven't used it (for) a while. I have to try it.

92. Do you know it/whether it will rain tomorrow? I was going to wash my car (tomorrow).

93. Tell me if/whether you are going to come. If you come, I will come too.

94. I don't know if/whether he/she has tried it/this. So, I don't know if/whether he/she likes it/this.

95. Can you tell me if/whether I look ok? How do I look?

96. I want to (/I'd like to) know if/whether I can pick it up tomorrow.

97. Do you know if/whether he/she speaks Korean?

98. I don't know if/whether I have to go, too. I don't want to (/wouldn't like to) go. But if I have to (go), I will (go).

99. I don't know if/whether we have done (/did) the right thing.

100. I want to/I'd like to know if/whether I have done (/did) something wrong.

Review

1. (My) Mom is busy preparing dinner.

2. We have to prepare dinner.

3. It took 3 hours to prepare (that).

4. I want to (/I'd like to) prepare for the test tonight.

5. I think we should prepare for the interview together.

6. I will prepare something.

7. I'm going to prepare lunch now.

8. I (have) prepared a cake.

9. He/She may/might prepare something for us.

10. I was going to prepare a (short) speech.

11. When I got/came home, mom was preparing dinner.

12. There is enough time to prepare for the test. / We (/I) have enough

time to prepare for the test.

13. I want to (/I'd like to) know how you prepared this.

14. We (have) prepared a surprise party for him. He is going to (/will) be surprised.

15. I don't know how I have to prepare for this test.

16. I haven't prepared (/didn't prepare) anything.

17. He hasn't prepared (/didn't prepare) for the test.

18. I (/We/You) don't have to prepare anything for it/that.

19. I'm not preparing for the/an interview. I haven't even started/begun it/ that yet.

20. It wasn't easy to prepare (this).

21. I couldn't prepare anything.

22. We are not preparing for the future. We have to do something about this/it.

23. It didn't take long to prepare this.

24. If you do that (/if you keep doing that), there isn't going to(/won't) be time to prepare anything later / you won't have time to prepare anything later.

25. I don't know if/whether he/she is preparing for the test.

26. What do you want to (/would you like to) prepare?

27. Everyone/Everybody is preparing something. What are we going to prepare?

28. What should I prepare?

29. Can we prepare for the test together?

30. Have you prepared for the/an interview? / Did you prepare for the/an interview?

31. Can you tell me what I have to prepare?

32. Are you preparing lunch? Do you need my help?

33. (If you were me,) How would you prepare for this? I want to (/I'd like to) know how you would prepare.

34. How were you going to prepare for this?

35. How did you prepare this alone/(all) by yourself?

36. What do we have to prepare? Do you know what we have to prepare?

37. Was there time to prepare this? / Did you have time to prepare this? Thank you for this/it. How long did it take to prepare this/it?

38. Hope for the best, but prepare for the worst.

39. We have to prepare for the worst.

40. I want to (/I'd like to) prepare for the worst.

41. It's a good idea to prepare for the worst.

42. We (have) already prepared for the worst.

43. Everyone/Everybody is preparing for the worst.

Unit 7

1. I know exactly what it/that is. Do you want to (/Would you like to) know what it is?

2. I can't(/don't) remember when it was.

3. I don't know how long it/that has been. It has been a few days.

4. I can't imagine how much it/this will be. I think it will be expensive.

5. I forgot where it used to be.

6. I want to (/I'd like to) know when it/that will be.

7. I wonder why you were sad. Can you tell me? You cried a lot.

8. I want to (/I'd like to) know how old you are. I don't want to (/I wouldn't like to) guess. Can you tell me how old you are?

9. I don't know where we are now. We might/may be lost.

10. I can't (/don't) remember what time it was.

11. Can you tell me what color it was?

12. I/We have to know how far it is. I want to (/I'd like to) go somewhere close/near.

13. I want to (/I'd like to) know when it/that will be ready.

14. Tell me where you have been. Where have you been?

15. Can (/Do) you remember how much it was? Did you spend a lot of money on it/that?

16. I wonder how he/she is. I haven't seen him/her for a long time.

17. I want to(/I'd like to) know how it/that was. Did you have a good/nice time?

18. Can you tell me how you have been? Have you been busy?

19. I wonder how it/that will be. It is going to(/will) be cool/nice/fantastic.

20. I forgot how much it used to be. The price used to be high.

21. I know where you were yesterday. You were in/at the park. I saw you there.

22. I'm not sure which way it will be. I/We have to ask someone/somebody.

23. I know who it/that is. Do you want to (/Would you like to) know who it is?

24. Can you tell me how long you have been here? Has it been long/ a long time?

25. I don't understand why I used to be scared/afraid of this/it. I used to be scared/afraid of a lot of (/many) things.

26. I don't know how long ago it was. It was a long time ago.

27. I don't know where he/she is from.

28. Can you tell me when he/she will be (/come) back to the office?

29. I wonder how many times you have been here.

30. I can't(/don't) remember how it/that used to be.

31. I want to (/I'd like to) know what size it (/this) is. Is it large? It looks small.

32. Tell me how good it was.

33. I don't know how big it used to be.

34. I/We have to know exactly what time it will be.

35. I wonder where he/she has been.

36. I don't know what time it is now. I don't have my phone now. I left it in the car.

37. Do you know how much these/they were?

38. Can you tell me where the bathroom/toilet is?

39. You don't know (/ You have no idea) how hard/difficult it was. You haven't tried/done it.

40. I can't imagine how hard/difficult it will be. But you can overcome it/this.

41. Tell me why you are late.

42. Do you know where you will (/are going to) be in 10 years from now?

43. Can you tell me where it/this was? Where did you find it?

44. I don't know where he/she is now. Do you know where he/she is? Where has he/she gone? / Where did he/she go?

45. I forgot which one it was.

46. I can't (/don't) remember which one it is. Which one is mine?

47. I don't know how old I was in this photo/picture. I was in my 20s.

48. Do you know whose car this/it is?

49. I wonder why it/this is here. Did you put it here?

50. Do you know why it/that was? I want to (/I'd like to) know the reason.

51. I want to (/I'd like to) know why it is like this. I haven't touched (/didn't touch) anything.

52. I know what you have been (/ what you were) worried about. But it (has) worked out (well). It's ok. Stop worrying about it/that.

53. I'm not sure how many times I've been there. I've been there many times (/a lot).

54. I don't know why I'm here. I came (/am) here for you. But I don't want to be/stay here.

55. I don't know why these/they are different. Can you explain what the difference is?

56. I understand why you were mad/angry. I want to (/I'd like to) apologize.

57. I wonder where my sunglasses are. Where did I put them? Do you know where they are?

58. I understand how hard/difficult it will be. It will (/is going to) be over soon. Be strong.

59. Tell me what your plan is (/your plans are). Do you have a plan B?

60. We have to know how it/that has been so far. We can change it. We can make it better.

61. Do you know if/whether he/she is married?

62. I wonder if/whether it was a lie. But there isn't a (/there is no) reason to lie.

63. I'm not sure if/whether I've been there.

64. I want to (/I'd like to) know if it/that will open tomorrow. Do I have to go today?

65. I don't know if/whether it is a good idea.

66. I wonder if/whether it was my fault.

67. Can you tell me if/whether it will be safe to swim here?

68. I want to (/I'd like to) know if/whether it was fun. Tell me everything. Don't leave anything out. /Leave out nothing.

69. I wonder if/whether it/that will be better. What should/shall I do?

70. Can you tell me if/whether these/they are the same? They look the same to me.

71. I want to (/I'd like to) know if/whether it is possible. Can you also tell me when it is possible?

72. I wonder if/whether it was possible.

73. Do you know if/whether it will be possible to do (that)?

74. I want to (/I'd like to) know if/whether it used to be possible. How was it (/did it use to be) possible?

75. I want to (/I'd like to) know if/whether you are ok. Are you ok? If you need someone to talk to, call me anytime.

76. I don't know if/whether he/she was ok. He looked/seemed worried.

77. I don't know if/whether he/she is busy now. He/She may/might be busy. When I see him/her, I will tell him/her.

78. I wonder if/whether it/this will end/finish soon. The sooner, the better.

79. I don't know if/whether it/this is the best. What do you think? What do you think we should do?

80. I want to (/I'd like to) know if/whether it/that was the best. Was there anything I could do?

81. Do you know if/whether there is a bank near/around here?

82. I have to know if/whether there was a problem. Was there a problem?

83. I want to (/I'd like to) know if/whether there will be enough time.

84. Tell me if/whether there is a possibility. If there is a possibility, I want to (/I'd like to) do something about it.

85. I don't know if/whether there was a reason. What was the reason?

86. I don't know if/whether there is a lot of traffic/a traffic jam.

87. Do you know if/whether there was a way?

88. Can you tell me if/whether there are a lot of(/many) people? How many people are there?

89. Tell me if/whether there were a lot of(/many) people. How many people were there?

90. I wonder if/whether there will be a lot of(/many) people. How many people will there be? The more, the better.

91. I don't know if/whether there is an ATM around/near here. I haven't seen it before. (/ I've never seen it.)

92. I don't know if/whether there was a problem at school. When he/she came/got home, something looked different.

93. I want to (/I'd like to) know if/whether there is a solution to this/it.

94. I don't know how many people there were. I didn't count.

95. Do you know how many people there will be? There will be thousands of people.

96. Can you tell me how many students there are in the class?

97. Do you know if/whether there are a lot of (/many) things to see? Is it a big city?

98. When it's over, I wonder if/whether there will be a chance to ask questions.

99. Can you tell me if/whether there is anything you want to do?

100. I want to (/I'd like to) know if/whether there is something I can do. I want to (/I'd like to) help.

Review

1. I will go out now.

2. We can go out now.

3. You have to go out now. Otherwise you are going to(/will) be late.

4. I might as well go out now, too.

5. As soon as you get here/come, we can go out.

6. I'm going out.

7. He/She has already gone out. / He/She already went out. / He/She went out already.

8. When I was coming in, he/she was going out.

9. I might/may go out with (my/some) friends tonight.

10. I used to go out every weekend.

11. He/She goes out every night. I wonder where he/she goes.

12. It's time to go out.

13. I was going to go out with my friends last night. But I couldn't (do that/ go out).

14. I wanted to go out with you. But I had to go somewhere. (I'm) Sorry.

15. I'm going to go out with (my/some) friends tonight. We ae going to (/will) have fun.

16. I don't want to (/wouldn't like to) go out.

17. I'm not going out now.

18. He doesn't go out much/often.

19. If you don't want (to), we don't have to go out.

20. I won't go out without you. I'll wait for you.

21. I don't think you should go out alone/by yourself.

22. He hasn't gone out yet.

23. I didn't go out yesterday. I didn't feel like it.

24. I wasn't going to go out yesterday. But he/she kept calling (me).

25. I haven't been out for a long time.

26. I don't know if/whether he/she has gone out (/ he/she went out).

27. You didn't use to go out every day.

28. We may/might not go out tonight.

29. I'm not going to go out today. I'm going to be/stay (at) home.

30. Can you tell me what time he went out?

31. Has Tim gone out? (/Did Tim go out?) When did he go out?

32. Do I have to go out, too?

33. Can I go out with (my/some) friends?

34. Shall we go out now?

35. Are you going out now? Where are you going?

36. (If you were me,) Would you go out with him/her?

37. When are you going to go out?

38. What time were you going to go out?

39. Can you tell me if/whether we can go out now?

40. Don't go out on a limb for me.

41. I went out on a limb for you.

42. You are going out on a limb.

43. You don't have to go out on a limb for me.

Unit 8

1. It's hard/difficult, isn't it? It's getting hard(er) (/more difficult).

2. It was a beautiful/lovely day, wasn't it? / The weather was good today, wasn't it?

3. It costs a lot (of money), doesn't it? I don't know if/whether I can afford (to do) it/that.

4. You like it/this, don't you?

5. I am right, aren't I? It didn't work out (well). I didn't want to be right. I wanted to be wrong.

6. You have been to China, haven't you? How was it? We might/may go to

China this summer.

7. I have to do it/this, don't I? I can do it now.

8. You were looking for it/this, weren't you? When I was cleaning(/ vacuuming the floor), I found it. It was under the sofa/couch.

9. There were a lot of (/many) people, weren't there?

10. You are going to come, aren't you? If you don't come, I am not going to (/ I won't) come, either.

11. It was an accident, wasn't it? You didn't do it on purpose. You didn't mean to do that/it, did you?

12. It/That looks dangerous, doesn't it? It doesn't look safe at all.

13. You have it/that, don't you?

14. I should fix it today, shouldn't I?

15. It took 3 days, didn't it?

16. You have been busy recently, haven't you?

17. I told you earlier, didn't I?

18. I am early, aren't I? There is a lot of time. (/ I have a lot of time.)

19. You are going to come/go with me, aren't you? (/ You will come/go with me, won't you?) You have to come. I don't want to go alone/by myself.

20. You were going to buy/get it/this, weren't you? I knew it/that.

21. You forgot, didn't you? How can you forget (about) that/it?

22. You know a lot about cars, don't you? I need (some) help.

23. Let's wait here, shall we?

24. Open the door, will you? Let me in.

25. He/she is here, isn't he/she? Where is he/she?

26. You already knew (it/that), didn't you? You always do that/it. You don't tell me anything. That/It is the problem.

27. You would go, wouldn't you? I don't know why I don't want to go this

time. I have to go, don't I?

28. There was a lot of traffic/a traffic jam, wasn't there? How long did it take to get/come here?

29. You saw it/this, didn't you? (/ You have seen this/it, haven't you?) It doesn't make sense, does it? It's so/really unfair.

30. I am pretty/beautiful, aren't I?

31. You had/ate lunch, didn't you? (/ You have had lunch, haven't you?) What did you have for lunch?

32. We have to hurry/rush, don't we?

33. It/That is increasing, isn't it?

34. Let's go, shall we?

35. We should go now, shouldn't we?

36. You regret it/that, don't you? But you don't have to regret it. You did your best. (/ You have done your best.) Everybody/Everyone knows (about) that/it.

37. There is a reason you didn't do (/you haven't done) it/this, isn't there? (/ You have a reason you didn't do it, don't you?) Can you tell me why you didn't do it?

38. I won, didn't I? I am (/feel/am feeling) so/very/really happy.

39. You were working, weren't you? I just came (here/by) to say hello. (/ I am just here to say hello.) See/Catch you later.

40. We are going to meet again soon, aren't we? (/ We will meet again soon, won't we?) Take care (of yourself).

41. We have to do something about it/that, don't we? It's getting (more) serious.

42. You wanted to have/get it/this, didn't you? (/You've wanted to have it, haven't you?)

43. It's far, isn't it? I think I should take my car.

44. We used to go there often, didn't we? (/ We often used to go there, didn't we?) Why did we stop going there? Do (/Can) you remember?

45. You would wait, wouldn't you? It's so/very/really hard/difficult to wait.

46. Stop it, will you?

47. You think he/she will like it/this, don't you?

48. I'm late, aren't I? I'm sorry. It/This won't happen again.

49. I am here, aren't I? You are not alone.

50. Let's meet next week, shall we? I will give you a call (/call (you)) next week.

51. I don't have to do this/it now, do I? I don't have time (now). (/ There isn't time (now)). When I can do it, I will (do it).

52. It's not true, is it? It's hard/difficult to believe.

53. You couldn't finish it/that yesterday, could you? I understand. You had a lot of/(so) many things to do (yesterday). (/ There were a lot of (/(so) many) things to do (yesterday)).

54. Don't say anything, will you? You have to promise me.

55. You haven't met him/her yet, have you?

56. You haven't told anyone/anybody, have you? (/ You didn't tell anyone/anybody, did you?) How did he/she know?

57. You are not using it/this, are you?

58. It doesn't matter, does it?

59. There wasn't anything (/There was nothing), was there?

60. You haven't been here long/for a long time, have you?

61. You aren't well, are you? (/ You don't feel well, do you? / You are not feeling well, are you?) You don't look well.

62. You don't know yet, do you?

63. There wasn't enough time, was there? (/ You didn't have enough time, did you?)

64. You are not going to tell anyone/anybody, are you? (/ You won't tell anyone/anybody, will you?)

65. It wasn't a/the problem, was it? I wonder what the problem was.

66. There wasn't a problem, was there? (/ You didn't have a problem, did you?)

67. It doesn't have to be big, does it? Will it/this fit?

68. You didn't want to come, did you? Thank you for coming.

69. You weren't going to come, were you? It was so/very/really nice/good to see you.

70. It won't take long, will it? (/ It's not going to take long, is it?)

71. It's not yours, is it? I wonder whose book it/this is.

72. You don't know where it/that is, do you? I wonder where it has gone (/ where it went).

73. We shouldn't tell him, should we? He will feel bad.

74. Don't be late, will you?

75. It won't happen again, will it? (/ It's not going to happen again, is it?)

76. You didn't like it, did you?

77. He/She doesn't play golf, does he/she?

78. We can't do it/this, can we?

79. I'm not helping, am I? I will get out of your way.

80. You aren't going to hang out with him/her, are you? (/ You won't hang out with him/her, will you?) Can you promise me (that)?

81. It's not getting better, is it? I thought so. (/ I knew it/that.)

82. You don't have time to help me, do you? (/ There isn't time to help me, is there?)

83. It doesn't take long, does it? I only have 10 minutes. (/ I have only 10

minutes.)

84. You didn't forget (about) it/that, did you?

85. You are not hungry yet, are you?

86. You don't think it will work, do you? If it doesn't work, what do I have to do?

87. Don't go, will you? Can you stay with me?

88. It's not too/that bad, is it?

89. There aren't a lot of (/many) people, are there?

90. You don't want to meet him/her, do you? (/You wouldn't like to meet him/her, would you?) I don't want to meet him/her, either.

91. It isn't working, is it? (/ It doesn't work, does it?)

92. You weren't talking about me, were you?

93. You don't remember, do you? (/You can't remember, can you?)

94. You weren't going to tell me, were you?

95. Don't think like that, will you?

96. You haven't been there yet, have you? I would go there this time.

97. There isn't anything I can do, is there?

98. It didn't cost much (money), did it?

99. I can't cancel it now, can I?

100. You weren't mad at/angry with me, were you?

Review

1. Have dinner with me today, will you?

2. I want to (/I'd like to) have dinner with you tomorrow. Is tomorrow ok?

3. We have to (/should) have dinner someday.

4. I can have dinner with you next week. See you next week.

5. I'm going to have dinner with a/my friend. Don't wait for me.

6. We should have dinner now.

7. I (have) already had dinner. (/ I had dinner already.)

8. We are having dinner. Do you want to (/Would you like to) join us?

9. I usually have dinner at 7.

10. When I got (t)here/arrived, they were having dinner.

11. We might as well have dinner here.

12. He/She used to come home to have dinner.

13. We might/may have dinner together after the show.

14. We were going to have dinner together. (But) He/She had to go back to work.

15. Let's have dinner together, shall we?

16. I don't want to (/wouldn't like to) have dinner with him/her.

17. I don't think we should have dinner now. It's a bit/a little (bit) early.

18. We aren't going to have dinner together today. I cancelled (it).

19. I haven't had dinner yet.

20. I couldn't have dinner with him/her.

21. I wasn't going to have dinner today. (But) Everything was delicious/yummy/yum.

22. You haven't had dinner, have you? (/ You didn't have dinner, did you?) Do you want to (/Would you like to) eat/have something now?

23. Until you get here/come, we/I won't have dinner.

24. He doesn't have dinner alone.

25. I'm not having dinner (now). It's too/very/so/really early.

26. I haven't had time to have dinner. (/ I didn't have time to have dinner.) I've been busy all day. (/ I was busy all day.)

27. We haven't had dinner together yet.

28. I don't know if/whether he/she (has) had dinner.

29. Do we have to have dinner now?

30. Where shall we have dinner?

31. Can you tell me what you want to (/you'd like to) have for dinner?

32. When are we going to have dinner together? Tell me now.

33. Do you want to (/Would you like to) have dinner with me?

34. Have you had dinner? (/ Did you have dinner?)

35. Are you having dinner (now)?

36. What time do you usually have dinner?

37. Was it good/nice to have dinner with him/her?

38. Were you having dinner?

39. Where do you think we should have dinner?

40. Can you tell me when you can have dinner with me?

41. Will there be a chance to have dinner with you again?

42. Where did you use to have dinner?

43. (If you were me,) Where would you have dinner?

Unit 9

1. I have been sleeping. I went to bed/sleep late last night. When did you get here/come?

2. I have been learning English for 2 years. It's fun to study English.

3. We have been living in this house since 2005. We used to live in Mapo before we moved here.

4. I have been working here for 4 years. It's already been 4 years. Time flies. (/Time is flying.)

5. Since he/she left school (/graduated), he/she has been working there.

6. I've been waiting since 2. Where were you?

7. Pam's been sleeping all morning.

8. Where have you been? Pam's been looking for you.

9. I've been looking for this/it. Thank you. Where did you find it?

10. I've been cleaning the house all day.

11. I'm tired. I've been sitting in the car for 3 hours.

12. My leg hurts/My legs hurt. I've been walking all day.

13. We've been studying hard today. I feel (/am feeling) good about it/that.

14. He/She has been working hard recently. He/She has been busy.

15. Jim's been watching TV since 1.

16. I've been thinking about you a lot recently.

17. We've been trying really/very/so hard. I don't know why they didn't choose us. We are going to (/will) win next time.

18. Tim's been teaching English for 6 years. He's a great teacher.

19. I've been using it/that for a long time. I can't use anything else.

20. I've been going there for a few months.

21. He/She has been talking for hours/a long time. It's boring.

22. I've been doing the housework.

23. I've been working out/exercising recently.

24. I've been calling you (/trying to call you) all day.

25. We've been talking about you.

26. I've been thinking about it/that. But I don't know what I have to do.

27. We have been doing something now. If it's ok, I will call you back soon.

28. I've been cooking for 2 hours.

29. He/She has been helping me. He/She is so/very/really nice, isn't he/she?

30. I'm tired. I've been driving for 3 hours. You are tired too, aren't you?

31. We've been studying English.

32. I've been driving this car for years (/a long time). I want to (/I'd like to)

buy/get a new car.

33. We've been listening to this song (for hours). I'm (getting) sick of (/tired of/sick and tired of) it. I want to (/I'd like to) listen to something else.

34. He/She's been looking for work/a job. It isn't easy to get/find a job these days.

35. Since he/she was 25 years old, he/she has been smoking. It is going to (/will) be hard/difficult to quit/stop.

36. Since I was little/a child/a kid, I've been doing it/this. It's easy.

37. I've been wondering about you. It's so/very/really nice/good to see you. How have you been?

38. Have you seen my white bag? (/ Did you see my white bag?) I've been looking for it all day. I can't find it anywhere. (/ It's nowhere. / It isn't anywhere.)

39. We've been working nonstop today. I want to (/I'd like to) know if we can take a break.

40. I've been taking a bus recently. I sold my/the car a month ago.

41. Long time no see. I've been meaning to call (you).

42. I'm sorry. I've been meaning to change it/that. I will do it now.

43. I've been meaning to do it/that. (But) there hasn't been (/wasn't) a chance to do that/it. (/ I haven't had (/didn't have) a chance to do that/it.)

44. I was going to contact/call you last week, (but) I'm sorry. I've been having a hard time.

45. You have been doing really/so/very well. I'm so/very/really proud of you.

46. You've been watching rom coms/romantic comedies a lot (/watching a lot of rom coms). It/That doesn't happen in real life.

47. I don't know who it is, but someone/somebody has been taking my paper. You don't know who it is, do you?

48. It's been raining all day. I love/like the sound of raindrops.

49. It's been snowing all night. Everything is white outside.

50. It's been snowing since Tuesday.

51. I haven't been doing anything.

52. I haven't been waiting that long. I got here/arrived (about) 10 minutes ago.

53. We haven't been talking about you.

54. I haven't been living here that long. I moved here last month.

55. He hasn't been working there long/for a long time.

56. I haven't been studying. I've been reading a book.

57. He/She hasn't been studying English long/for a long time.

58. We haven't been talking/speaking to each other for a few days. When he/she is angry/mad, he/she doesn't talk/speak. It's really/very/so annoying.

59. I haven't been thinking about him/her for a while.

60. I haven't been doing much.

61. I haven't been going there for a few months.

62. I haven't been sleeping. I've been meditating.

63. I haven't been feeling good recently. I've been feeling down.

64. I haven't been sleeping well recently. I am exhausted/tired.

65. We haven't been dating long/for a long time. We first met last month. It's been a month.

66. I haven't been staying here that long. It's been 3 days. I am going to go back to Korea next week.

67. We haven't been listening to this song for a long time/long. It/This used to be our favorite song.

68. I haven't been drinking for a few days. I (have) decided to quit/stop

drinking.

69. I haven't been using it/this for a while. I don't know if/whether it works (/is working).

70. I haven't been working out/exercising for a few months. I am going to go (back) to the gym from next month.

71. What have you been doing?

72. How long have you been working here?

73. How long have you been studying English? You speak English well (/ You speak good English).

74. What have you been thinking about? Have you been thinking about me?

75. How long have you been living here? When did you move here?

76. I'm sorry I'm late. Have you been waiting long/for a long time?

77. How long have you been waiting? When did you get here/come?

78. What have you been doing all day?

79. How long have you been using it/this?

80. Have you been going there long/for a long time? How long has it been?

81. Have you been talking about me? I want to (/I'd like to) know what you have been talking about.

82. Have you been watching a movie? Is it a good movie?

83. This car looks old. Have you been driving this car long/for a long time?

84. Have you been sleeping? You sound sleepy.

85. How long have you been working with him? Do you know him well?

86. What have you been making?

87. How long have you been doing it/this? You do it/this well. (/ You are doing it/this well.)

88. How long has Tim been teaching English? Does he have a lot of

experience?

89. Have you been doing something? Did I disturb/interrupt (you)? If you want, I can come back later.

90. Have I been doing well?

91. Your eyes are red (/Your eye is red). Have you been crying? What's up?

92. Have you been drinking? Are you ok?

93. You are out of breath. Have you been running?

94. You are sweating. Have you been working out/exercising?

95. Have you been waiting for me? Is there something you want to tell me? / Do you have something to tell me?

96. Have you been singing?

97. It's been a long time (/a while) since I last saw you. What have you been doing?

98. Have you been using my (cell/mobile) phone? How did you unlock my phone?

99. Have you been reading my email(s)? It's an invasion of privacy.

100. Has it been raining?

Review

1. I can work tomorrow.

2. I am going to work this weekend. There is a project I have to finish.

3. I have to work tomorrow, don't I?

4. We are working together. We are doing a project together.

5. We might/may work together tomorrow.

6. I used to work here, too.

7. I worked yesterday.

8. We might as well work together.

9. He/She works very/really/so hard. He/She works 7 days a week.

10. I was going to work last weekend (too), but there was a seminar I had to attend.

11. When I got here/came, everyone/everybody was already working (/ everyone was working already).

12. I think we should work together. So, we can finish early.

13. I've been working here for 2 years. (/ I've worked here for 2 years.)

14. You have been working now, haven't you? Don't mind me.

15. I don't know if/whether he/she will work this weekend.

16. I don't want to (/wouldn't like to) work with him/her.

17. I'm not going to work tomorrow. I'm free tomorrow. Is there something you want to do?

18. I can't work here anymore/any longer.

19. He didn't use to work hard. He (has) changed a lot.

20. We may/might not work together.

21. I don't think we should work tonight. Everybody/Everyone is tired. Let's begin/start tomorrow, shall we?

22. I didn't work last weekend.

23. I couldn't work yesterday. I wasn't (feeling) well. (/ I didn't feel well.)

24. I haven't been working here long/for a long time. (/ I haven't worked here long.) I began/started 2 months ago.

25. I don't know how many hours I worked yesterday.

26. You aren't working now, are you? There is something I have to tell you.

27. Where do you work?

28. Do you/I have to work tomorrow?

29. Can you tell me when you can work?

30. Did you work yesterday? How many hours did you work?

31. How long have you been working here? (/ How long have you worked

here?) Has it been long/a long time?

32. Before you came here, where did you use to work?

33. Where are you going to work tomorrow?

34. Why do you want to (/would you like to) work here? Why is this/it your dream job?

35. Are you working (now)? Where are you working?

36. Can I work with you? I've always wanted to work with you.

37. Work it out between you two.

38. At first, we didn't see eye to eye, (/ We didn't see eye to eye at first,) but we worked it out together.

39. When we first met, we used to fight (/fought) a lot. But we worked it out. Our relationship is good now.

40. We can work it/this out together.

41. I (have) worked it/that out.

42. We are working it/that out together now.

Unit 10

1. Do you mind if I sit here? There isn't anywhere to sit. (/ There is nowhere to sit.)

2. Do you mind if I take it/this?

3. Do you mind if I tell him/her? He/She has to know, too.

4. Do you mind if I see (/look at/have a look at/take a look at) it/that? I have to see it with my own (two) eyes.

5. Do you mind if I ask a personal question? I've been meaning to ask this question. It is a good chance to ask my question.

6. Do you mind if I leave it open (for a while)?

7. Do you mind if I call you back later? I'm in the middle of something (now).

8. Do you mind if I reschedule?

9. Do you mind if I give it back (to you)/ return it tomorrow?

10. Do you mind if I let you know tomorrow? I haven't decided (it) yet.

11. Do you mind if I come back in 5 minutes? I'll be/come back soon.

12. Do you mind if I choose/pick this/it?

13. Do you mind if I open it/this? I want to (/I'd like to) know what is in it.

14. Do you mind if I leave/put it/this there?

15. Do you mind if I join (you)?

16. Do you mind if I go/come with you?

17. Do you mind if I go/leave now? It's ok, isn't it?/You don't mind, do you?

18. Do you mind if I keep it/this? I might/may need it later.

19. Do you mind if I pay you back tomorrow?

20. Do you mind if I redo it/this?

21. Do you mind if I talk/speak to my family first? After I talk/speak to my family, I want to (/I'd like to) decide.

22. Do you mind if I think about it? I can't decide (it) right now. I need time to think (about it).

23. Do you mind if I talk/speak to him/her for a minute? It isn't going to (/ won't) be/take long.

24. Do you mind if I lie down for a minute? I am (/feel/am feeling) dizzy.

25. Do you mind if I take it/this home?

26. Do you mind if I speak Korean for a minute? My friend doesn't speak English. I want to/I'd like to explain it/this to him/her.

27. Do you mind if I take/have a sip?

28. Do you mind if I pick this/it up later (/come back later to pick it up)?

29. Do you mind if I have/eat this sandwich? I haven't eaten/had anything all day. Do you want to (/would you like to) have/eat some?

30. Do you mind if I take this call/answer this? I've been waiting for this (phone) call.

31. Would you mind if I used your phone? My phone is dead.

32. Would you mind if I left 5 minutes early today?

33. Would you mind if I said something?

34. Would you mind if I took a look around (/looked around)?

35. Would you mind if I took this chair? Are you using it/this?

36. Would you mind if I picked it/that up tomorrow? I don't have time today.

37. Would you mind if I dropped it/that off the day after tomorrow?

38. Would you mind if I came a (little) bit late? I might/may be a (little) bit (/a little) late.

39. Would you mind if I tasted it/this? It looks delicious/yummy/yum. It smells delicious/yummy, too.

40. Would you mind if I wrote it/that (down)?

41. Would you mind if I tried it/this?

42. Would you mind if I copied it/this?

43. Would you mind if I did it later? I don't have time now. As soon as I can, I will (do it).

44. Would you mind if I left it/this on?

45. Would you mind if I took my time? I don't want to (/wouldn't like to) hurry/rush.

46. Would you mind if I mixed it/this?

47. Would you mind if I closed/shut this/it?

48. Would you mind if I invited my friend?

49. Would you mind if we talked about (/discussed) it/this later?

50. Would you mind if I uploaded/posted this picture/photo?

51. Do you mind checking it/that again (/rechecking it/that)?

52. Do you mind doing it/this?

53. There is a problem with my iPad. (/ I have a problem with my iPad.) Do you mind having(/taking) a look at it?

54. There is a problem with my car. (/ I have a problem with my car.) Do you mind helping (me)?

55. Do you mind showing me?

56. Do you mind waiting? I'll be/come back soon.

57. Do you mind picking me up on the/your way there?

58. Do you mind watching my bag for a minute?

59. Do you mind sharing your/the recipe?

60. I left my scarf there. Do you mind looking for it?

61. Do you mind turning it down a (little) bit (/a little)?

62. Do you mind cutting it/this in half?

63. Do you mind calling (me/us) first before you come next time?

64. Do you mind telling me why you haven't done it/this yet?

65. Do you mind leaving it/that closed?

66. Do you mind helping me with it/this?

67. Do you mind stopping here for a minute?

68. Do you mind explaining it/that to me?

69. Do you mind getting that/it?

70. Do you mind answering (my question)?

71. Would you mind printing it/this (out)?

72. Would you mind doing this/it first? (/Would you mind working on this first?)

73. Would you mind turning/switching it/that off?

74. Would you mind handing me the remote (control)?

75. Would you mind packing your bag now? We are going to leave

tomorrow. I think you should pack (your bag) now.

76. Would you mind unpacking your bag in your/the room?
77. Would you mind helping me (to) load?
78. Would you mind helping me (to) unload?
79. Would you mind holding it/this?
80. Would you mind slowing down?
81. Would you mind wiping it/that?
82. Would you mind moving your car?
83. Would you mind giving me more time?
84. Would you mind coming closer?
85. Would you mind closing your eyes?
86. Would you mind feeling my forehead? Do I have a fever?
87. Would you mind removing the stain (/getting rid of the stain)?
88. Would you mind sitting next to me? I don't want to (/wouldn't like to) be alone now.
89. Dinner's almost/nearly ready. Would you mind setting the table?
90. Would you mind writing it/that (down) here? I don't know what that/it means.
91. I don't mind waiting. Take your time.
92. I don't mind standing here. Don't worry about me.
93. I don't mind going alone. You don't have to come along.
94. I don't mind eating here. If you want to eat here, we can (do that).
95. I don't mind sitting here.
96. I don't mind helping him/her. He/She needs our help.
97. I don't mind doing this/it. I like doing it/this. I'm glad/happy to help.
98. If you don't want to drive now, I don't mind driving.
99. I don't mind staying/being here. But, if you want to (/you'd like to) go

somewhere else, we can (do that).

100. I don't mind sleeping on the sofa/couch. Thanks for letting me stay here.

Review

1. I will look for it. If/When I find it, I'll call (you) right away.

2. We have to look for that/it.

3. You are looking for something (now), aren't you? What is it?

4. When I go/get home, I can look for it for you.

5. I was going to look for it when I came home yesterday. But I forgot.

6. He/She might/may look for you.

7. I want to (/I'd like to) look for it now.

8. I've been looking for my white bag all morning. Have you seen it? (/ Did you see it?)

9. (If I were you), I would look for a solution.

10. We should look for it together.

11. I (have) looked for it/that everywhere. (/ I looked everywhere for it/that.) But I couldn't find it. I (have) lost it.

12. I've been looking for it/this. (/ I was looking for it/this.) Thanks. Where did you find it?

13. There are a lot of (/(so)many) things here. I can't look for it/that here.

14. We don't have to look for it/that. We don't need it.

15. I am not looking for anything.

16. I can't (/don't) remember if/whether I looked for it there (/looked there for it).

17. I'm never going to look for it again. (/ I'm not going to look for it (ever) again.)

18. I couldn't look for it/that last night. (I'm) Sorry.

19. I don't want to (/wouldn't like to) look for it/that. It's a waste of time.

20. He wasn't looking for me, was he? (/ He didn't look for me, did he?)

21. You shouldn't look for me again.

22. Don't look for me.

23. Are you going to look for it/that? When are you going to do that/it?

24. Where should we look (for it)?

25. Is there something you are looking for?

26. Shall we look for it together?

27. I left it/that there. Can/Could/Would you look for it?

28. Can you tell me what you are looking for?

29. Have you looked for it? (/ Did you look for it?)

30. Can/Could/May I look for it?

31. Were you looking for something? (/ Have you been looking for something?)

32. Do you mind if I look for it/that? (/ Would you mind if I looked for it? / Is it ok if I look for it?)

33. Do I have to look for it/that? Do I have to have it?

34. It's like a needle in a haystack.

35. It was like looking for a needle in a haystack. It was impossible.

36. We are looking for a needle in a haystack.

기초영어 1000문장 말하기 연습 3

2020년 6월 16일 초판 1쇄 발행
2020년 6월 23일 초판 2쇄 발행

지 은 이 | 박미진
펴 낸 이 | 서장혁
기획편집 | 이경은
디 자 인 | 정인호
마 케 팅 | 한승훈, 최은성, 한아름

펴 낸 곳 | 토마토출판사
주   소 | 경기도 파주시 회동길 216 2층
T E L | 1544-5383
홈페이지 | www.tomato4u.com
E-mail | support@tomato4u.com
등   록 | 2012. 1. 11.
I S B N | 979-11-90278-30-0 (14740)